THE FEDERAL COMMUNICATIONS COMMISSION, THE BROADCAST INDUSTRY, AND THE FAIRNESS DOCTRINE 1981-1987

Donald J. Jung

University Press of America, Inc.
Lanham • New York • London

Copyright © 1996 by
University Press of America,® Inc.
4720 Boston Way
Lanham, Maryland 20706

3 Henrietta Street
London, WC2E 8LU England

Library of Congress Cataloging-in-Publication Data

Jung, Donald J.
The Federal Communications Commission, the broadcast industry,
and the fairness doctrine, 1981-1987 / Donald J. Jung.
p.   cm.
Includes bibliographical references and index.
l. Fairness doctrine (Broadcasting)--United States--History. 2.
United States. Federal Communications Commission--History. I.
Title.
KF2812.J86   1996   343.7309'94 --dc20   96-20845 CIP
(347.303994)

ISBN 0-7618-0436-6 (cloth: alk. ppr.)

♾™ The paper used in this publication meets the minimum
requirements of American National Standard for information
Sciences—Permanence of Paper for Printed Library Materials,
ANSI Z39.48—1984

Contents

PREFACE

The broadcast fairness doctrine is past. It was a reflection of history, conditions and players no longer joined as they were. It seems as though one of the first questions I am often asked is whether I support the fairness doctrine. Answering this question has always been problematic because it was never what intrigued me about the doctrine, its application and implementation in the first place. What has always fascinated me about the doctrine was that it was an imperfect attempt to meld private, public and political interests. So instead of answering the question directly, I've usually chosen to respond by saying that the doctrine illustrates nicely the myth of journalistic ethics in the real-world conflict with commercial activity and political advantage. The fairness doctrine did not exist first. Problems existed first and the doctrine was an acknowledgment of their existence.

The doctrine acknowledged that print and electronic media are not identical. I have the greatest respects for journalists whether print or electronic. But what journalists do, and what the organizations which give them their platforms of expression do are not always complimentary. Commercial media interests exist to make a profit and the news provided by journalists is just one product for these commercial endeavors. Righteousness aside, a study of the dynamics of interested parties surrounding the fairness doctrine debate in the 1980's is interesting and worthwhile in and of itself. That is what I attempt to do here. Not surprisingly the most vocal players at the time were a Federal Communications Commission driven by a mix of conservative and libertarian ideologies, and self-interested commercial broadcast and advertising interests. I draw heavy on these interests own rhetoric because they had the most readily available forums to make their views heard, not because I believe them. Nor do I believe just because a group has the moniker of being a public interest group it reflects an interest which is purely public.

Though times and conditions are different today than they were in 1987, the importance of reasoned public discussion of the idea of access is every bit as relevant today. I believe this case study illustrates well how difficult reasoned public discussion is when legislative mandates as weak and ambiguous, politics takes precedence over substance, independent agencies are driven by their own agendas, and private interests are more than willing to articulate what constitutes public interest (which just coincidentally meets their own private interest).

I owe a special debt of gratitude to Professor David Berg at Purdue University for his insight and patience with this project in its formative stages, and Professor Andrew Calabrese at the University of Colorado for his critical insight. Also, I need to acknowledge the support and encouragement I have gotten for this project from Professors Thomas McPhail and Michael Murray at the University of Missouri-St. Louis, as well as financial support received from the University of Missouri Research Board.

INTRODUCTION

On Tuesday, August 4, 1987, the Federal Communications Commission (FCC), in one bold stroke, declared it would no longer enforce the 38-year-old broadcast fairness doctrine.[1] Ironically, in its demise it had for the first time in its history attained status as a major popular news story. Prior to this event, discussion about the broadcast fairness doctrine had been the subject of extensive academic and legal debate. This academic and legal debate had focussed primarily on social, economic, and constitutional issues. The fairness doctrine had also been the focus of extended coverage in the broadcast industry trade press. But on this day stories about the controversial FCC ruling appeared on all of the TV network evening newscasts, was carried live on C-Span, was the subject of numerous radio reports, and appeared on the front pages of many newspapers nationwide.

What was the broadcast fairness doctrine, and how had it come to finally attain "star" status? On one level, the answer to the first part of this question is simple. The fairness doctrine was an administrative rule that placed a two part obligation upon broadcast licensees: first, broadcasters had an obligation to cover vitally important controversial issues of interest in their communities; second, broadcasters were obligated to provide a reasonable opportunity for the presentation of contrasting viewpoints on those controversial issues of public importance they covered.

On a more abstract level, though, the answer to the first part of the above question, what is the broadcast fairness doctrine, is anything but simple. Discussion of the doctrines meaning on this level has provided, and continues to provide, politicians, policymakers, economists, academicians, and public interest advocates literally hundreds of opportunities for interpretation and conjecture. The focus of this investigation is the lesser studied second part of the above question. That is, how had an obscure governmental regulation come to achieve the status of a major news story?

Much scholarship has focused on either the correctness or incorrectness of the commission's 1987 decision eliminating its enforcement of the doctrine. Though vitally significant, such analysis has failed to provide a solid historical chronology of how the FCC systematically positioned itself between 1981 and 1987 to achieve this end. Developing such a historical chronology is what is proposed here.

Specifically, this study seeks to provide an institutional history of the FCC during this period--a study organized chronologically, and based on documentary research and interviews. Because this study focuses on regulatory reform, Roger Noll's four-part typology[2] will be used as a means of organizing this material.

For Noll, regulatory reform can be affected through four different means: (1) reorganization, (2) procedural reform, (3) changing the mandate, and (4) altering the external environment. These strategies for achieving regulatory reform can be used individually or in combination. And each one has a unique purpose. The assumption underlying reorganization proposals is that the location of regulatory responsibility within the governmental hierarchy and the organizational structure of the administering agency significantly affect policy outcomes. Analysis of procedural reforms is necessary because administrative law, legal precedent, and the operating rules adopted by agencies determine the flow of information into administrative proceedings and, in principle, constrain the decision-making power of agencies. Noll's third type of reform proposal, that of changing the mandate, centers on the objectives, methods, and powers given to agencies by Congress through legislation and, to a lesser degree, by the President through executive order. Noll believes if agencies adopt bad policies or overlook key issues, one possible remedy lies in clarifying or correcting the mandate. The final type of reform proposal identified by Noll is altering the external environment. If the interactions among an agency, a particular industry, or groups with a stake in the industry's performance, the courts, and/or Congress produce unsatisfactory results, one approach to reform is to restructure these external institutions so that the agency is better able to produce the desired performance. The FCC during the period investigated effected change in each of these four broad areas. This study traces these changes in their historical context.

Previous historical studies of the Federal Communications Commission have focused on its role in the establishment and implementation of content-based broadcast regulation. A sampling of these include Ford Rowan's *Broadcast Fairness*,[3] Steven Simmons' *The Fairness Doctrine and the Media*,[4] Barry Cole and Mal Oettinger's *Reluctant Regulators*,[5] and James Baughman's *Television's Guardians: The FCC and the Politics of Programming 1958-1967*.[6]

The first two of these, Rowan's *Broadcast Fairness* and Simmons' *The Fairness Doctrine and the Media*, though useful for providing reference for the proposed study, are more concerned with developing an intellectual history, and therefore do not function as a model on which an institutional history can be based. Cole et al., and Baughman do focus more on the institutional side. Baughman's *Television's Guardians*, in particular, seems a workable model. Baughman, who is currently at the University of Wisconsin, provides first a historical review of the FCC, and then focuses on two "crises," one regulatory and the other cultural, which provide a frame for him to begin his study of the commission between 1958 and 1967. Finally, Baughman traces historically some of the complex processes which occurred at the FCC during this period, and interprets their social, political, economic, and technological effects.

The FCC during the period 1958 to 1967 shares many similarities with the commission between 1981 and 1987. Though these commissions are ideologically distinct, many of the internal conflicts and external pressures affecting them are quite similar. Both commissions were chaired by strong ideologues unafraid to vigorously advocate their positions--Newton Minow in 1961 and Mark Fowler in 1981. Both commissions had to contend with Congressional action designed to undermine its authority and effectiveness. And, finally, both commissions had to contend not only with their own predetermined workloads, but also with a political change in administration. In 1960 this change in administration was from Republican Eisenhower to Democrat Kennedy, and in 1980 from Democrat Carter to Republican Reagan.

Using Baughman's *Television's Guardians* as a model for studying the current commission offers several distinct advantages. First, Baughman's method of research is sound. It is based on both documentary evidence and interviews with relevant individuals. The current study does the same.

Organization of Study

This historical study is arranged chronologically. The research method is similar to that used by Baughman. It consists of interviews with individuals within the commission during this period, as well as individuals who had cause to interact with the commission then. Additional material was gathered through congressional testimony, commission proceedings, legal findings, and contemporaneous press accounts.

The study is organized into seven major sections. The Introduction includes the rationale for the study, the primary research question, and methodological and literature review. Chapter I includes a brief overview and history of both the FCC and the broadcast fairness doctrine. Chapter II gives a historical context of the period between the 1969 *Red Lion*[7] decision until the election of Ronald Reagan in 1980, and his appointment of Mark Fowler as chairman of the FCC in 1981. Chapter III focuses on actions taken by the commission between 1981-1983, culminating in the release of the its 1983 Fairness Doctrine Inquiry. Chapter IV focuses on actions taken by the commission between 1983-1985, culminating in the release of its 1985 Fairness Doctrine Report. Chapter V focuses on the commission's activity germane to the broadcast fairness doctrine between 1985-1987, culminating in its August 4, 1987, decision to cease enforcement of the doctrine. Chapter V also provides a brief postscript on activities undertaken by the commission, Congress, and the courts during the remainder of 1987 and through to the departure of Ronald Reagan in 1988. Chapter VI provides an analysis and conclusions.

NOTES

[1] In Re Complaint of Syracuse Peace Council Against Television Station WTVH, Syracuse, New York. Memorandum Opinion and Order. 2 FCC Rcd 5045. recon. denied, 3 FCC Rcd 2035 (1988). Adopted August 4, 1987. Released August 6, 1987.

[2] Noll, Roger G. 1982. *Regulatory Policy and the Social Sciences.* Berkeley, CA: University of California Press. pp. 12-14.

[3] Rowan, Ford. *Broadcast Fairness: Doctrine, Practice, Prospects.* 1984. New York: Longman.

[4] Simmons, Steven. *The Fairness Doctrine and the Media.* 1978. Berkeley, CA: University of California Press.

[5] Cole, Barry, and Mal Oettinger. *Reluctant Regulators: The FCC and the Broadcast Audience.* 1978. Reading, MA: Addison-Wesley Publishing.

[6] Baughman, James L. 1985. *Television's Guardians: The FCC and the Politics of Programming 1958-1967.* Knoxville, Tenn.: University of Tennessee Press.

[7] *Red Lion Broadcasting Co. v. Federal Communications Commission,* 395 U.S. 367 (1969).

CHAPTER I

OVERVIEW AND HISTORY OF THE FEDERAL COMMUNICATIONS COMMISSION AND THE FAIRNESS DOCTRINE PRIOR TO 1981

Overview and History of the FCC

The Federal Communications Commission was formally created as a result of the Communications Act of 1934.[1] Historically it has served as a government organization delegated the responsibility for the development and implementation of much U.S. communications policy. Commercial broadcasting policy, a particular aspect of U.S. communications policy, has a rich and varied history. But no study can ignore that the history of commercial broadcasting in the U.S. is one based on government regulation. The airwaves used by commercial broadcasters have historically been viewed as a public resource available to individuals, but subject to necessary rules for orderly and efficient use. For this reason, it is often argued that commercial broadcasters are obligated to perform certain public trustee functions in exchange for use of a public resource.

The historical basis of the broadcast fairness doctrine, that of serving the public interest, predates the history of the FCC itself. In 1910, for example, Congress passed legislation placing telegraph, telephone, and cable companies doing interstate business under the jurisdiction of the Interstate Commerce Commission. That same year, president William H. Taft signed the Radio Act of 1910 governing radio communications concerning safety of life at sea. Passage of the Radio Act of 1910 was made necessary as a result of unrestricted use of wireless telegraph and telephone, and to the extent that they were interfering with public and private message transmission, including calls from vessels in distress. The limits placed on users of the radio spectrum by the Radio Act were deemed as necessary controls to maintain order. As such, these restrictions were deemed to be in the public interest. The Federal Radio Act was passed in 1927[2] and, among other things, created the Federal Radio Commission as an independent agency controlling broadcasting and other radio activities for one year.[3] The Department of Commerce assumed radio licensing authority in 1928, and in 1930 Congress made the Federal Radio Commission permanent. The public interest standard, in the context of radio broadcasting, gained some specificity in 1932. That year the U.S. Supreme Court upheld a provision of the Radio Act of 1927 declaring air channels to be public property.[4]

In 1934 Congress passed the Communications Act creating the bipartisan Federal Communications Commission. The new Federal Communications Commission was charged not only with regulating radio, but also cable, telegraph, and telephone systems. For all practical purposes, this change in administrative machinery resulting from the 1934 Act made little difference to the already established relations between the federal regulatory authority and the radio industry. In fact, the sections of the 1934 Act dealing with the radio industry substantially reproduced the 1927 Act. Since 1934, amendments have been made to the original Communications Act, but these amendments have related mainly to procedural matters with negligible affect on the Act's main structure. The system of federal regulation as it exists today, then, is essentially that which had been established in 1927.

Overview and History of the Fairness Doctrine

Initial commission attempts to influence programming met with little opposition, except on two occasions. The first came as a result of a 1940 suit brought against the commission by the Mayflower Broadcasting Company.[5] Here, a Boston station had broadcast editorials urging the election of certain candidates for public office and expressing views on controversial questions. The commission had criticized the station for doing this and renewed its license only after receiving assurances that the stations would no longer broadcast editorials. The resulting court determination held that the commission was indeed acting within its authority in promulgating such policy. This ban on broadcast editorials became known as the *Mayflower* doctrine.

Such a broad editorial ban soon proved unrealistic. And it led to a different approach to be taken by the commission with respect to program regulation. In 1948 the commission re-examined the question of program regulation and on June 2, 1949, issued a 13-page report which, while not explicitly repudiating the *Mayflower* doctrine, nevertheless expressed approval of editorializing. However, editorial-izing by licensees was now subject to the criterion of "overall fairness."[6] Though the commission agreed that its ruling involved an abridgment of freedom, it believed this abridgment was necessary. As the commission stated:

> The most significant meaning of freedom of the radio is the right of the American people to listen to this great medium of communications free from any governmental dictation as to what they can or cannot hear and free alike from similar restraints by private licensees.[7]

The commission mandated broadcast licensees to devote a reasonable percentage of their broadcasting time to the discussion of public issues. The commission reasoned this would give the public a reasonable opportunity to hear different opposing positions on the public issues of interest and importance in their community.

Most agree this 1949 commission report formalized an administra-tive policy that became known as the fairness doctrine. This policy established a twofold duty for broadcasters. First, broadcasters must give adequate coverage to public issues.[8] Second, coverage must be fair in that it accurately reflects the opposing views.[9] The language in the 1934 Communications Act requiring that broadcast regulation serve the public interest was used as justification for this decision.

Congress amended the Communications Act in 1959 to specifically exempt newscasts from a requirement that broadcasters provide political candidates with equal opportunities for air time. Concerned that this might be misconstrued as a weakening of the fairness standard, Congress in 1959 added language stating that the exemption did not relieve broadcasters of the obligation to act in the public interest "and to afford reasonable opportunity for the discussion of conflicting views on issues of public importance."[10] This language is what many believed codified the fairness doctrine.

The fairness doctrine withstood a first amendment challenge in the 1969 *Red Lion Broadcasting*[11] decision. The U.S. Supreme Court, by a 7-0 vote, ruled that the FCC had acted within its authority in promulgating the fairness doctrine. "Where there are substantially more individuals who want to broadcast than there are frequencies to allocate," the court said, "it is idle to posit an unabridgeable first amendment right to broadcast comparable to the right of every individual to speak, write or publish."[12] Following both Congressional and Supreme Court approval of the fairness doctrine, most assumed that it firmly was established and codified as part of the Communications Act. Most broadcasters complied with the doctrine, and some stations prided themselves in providing free time for contrasting views.

In 1974 the FCC issued another Fairness Report.[13] It again explicitly stated that broadcasters had a two-pronged obligation: (1) broadcast licensees were required to provided coverage of vitally important controversial issues of interest in the community served; and (2), to provide a reasonable opportunity for the presentation of contrasting viewpoints of such issues.

And as late as 1981, the right of the audience to have access to ideas, rather than an absolute first amendment right of the broadcasters to speak, was again reinforced. In *CBS v. F.C.C.*[14] the Supreme Court ruled that the right of access to the broadcast media does not violate first amendment rights of broadcasters by unduly limiting their editorial discretion. Rather, the Court found, that the right of access to the broadcast media balances the rights of broadcasters, candidates, and the public. Ironically, also in 1981, the new Fowler FCC recommended to Congress the repeal of the fairness doctrine, the equal opportunities doctrine, and the reasonable access law.[15]

Notes

[1] 47 CFR Ch. 1 Part 0. Federal Communications Commission. Washington, DC: U.S. Government Printing Office. 1987. pp.i-vii,1-85.

[2] Radio Act of 1927, Section 4, 44 Stat 116.

> The Federal Radio Commission was established to allocate frequencies among competing applicants in a manner responsive to the public "convenience, interest, or necessity."

[3] Before 1927, the allocation of frequencies was left entirely to the private sector, and the result was chaos. Because of this chaos, a series of National Radio Conferences was held between 1922 and 1925, at which it was resolved that regulation of the radio spectrum by the Federal Government was essential and that regulatory power should be utilized to ensure that allocation of this limited resource would be made only to those who would serve the public interest. The 1923 Conference expressed the opinion that the Radio Communications Act of 1912, 37 Stat 302, conferred upon the Secretary of Commerce the power to regulate frequencies and hours of operation, but when Secretary Hoover sought to implement this claimed power the Federal Appeals Court for the District of Columbia held the 1912 Act not to permit enforcement.

[4] *Great Lakes Broadcasting Company v. Federal Radio Commission*, 3 FRC. Ann.Rep. 32-33 (1929), rev'd on other grounds, 37 F.2d 993 (D.C.Cir. 1930), cert. dismissed, 281 U.S. 706 (1930).

[5] *Mayflower Broadcasting Corp. v. FCC*, 8 FCC 333 (1940).

[6] *Editorializing by Broadcast Licensees*, 13 FCC 1246 (1949).

[7] Ibid., at 1257.

[8] *United Broadcasting Co. v. FCC*, 10 FCC 515 (1945).

[9] *New Broadcasting Co. v. FCC*, 6 P&F Radio Reg 258 (1950).

[10] Act of September 14, 1959, Section 1, P.L. 66-274, 73 Stat 557, amending 47 USC Section 315(a).

> The 1959 amendment to the Communications Act of 1934 amended the statutory requirement of Section 315 that equal time be accorded each political candidate to except certain appearances on news programs, but added that this constituted no exception "from the obligation imposed upon them under the Act to operate in the public interest and to afford reasonable opportunity for the discussion of conflicting views on issues of public importance." The language makes it very plain the Congress, in 1959, announced that the phrase "public interest," which had been in the Act since 1927, imposes a duty on

broadcasters to discuss both sides of controversial public issues. In other words, the amendment vindicated the FCC's general view that the fairness doctrine inhered in the public interest standard.

[11]*Red Lion Broadcasting Co. v. FCC*, 395 U.S. 367 (1969).

[12]Ibid., at 388.

[13]*Fairness Report* in Docket No. 19260, 48 FCC 2d 1 (1974), recon. denied, 58 FCC 2d 691 (1976), aff'd sub nom *National Citizens Committee for Broadcasting v. FCC*, 567 F.2d 1095 (D.C. Cir. 1977) cert. denied, 436 U.S. 926 (1978) ["1974 Fairness Report"].

[14]*Columbia Broadcasting System, Inc. v. F.C.C.*, 453 U.S. 367 (1981).

[15]*Revision of Applications for Renewal of License of Commercial and Non-Commercial AM, FM, and Television Stations.* Report and Order in BC Docket No. 80-253. 46 Fed.Reg 26236 (May 11, 1981).

To understand that doing away with these provisions were part of an agenda which Mark Fowler brought to his chairmanship of the commission see: Fowler, Mark and Daniel Brenner, "A marketplace approach to broadcast regulation." 60 *Texas Law Review* 2, pp.145-200 (1982); Fowler, Mark, Albert Halprin and James D. Schlichting, "'Back to the Future': A Model for Telecommunications." *Federal Communications Law Journal.* 38:2. 1986. pp.145-200; and, Fowler, Mark. "Address before the International Radio Television Society. Reprinted in Mark Fowler, "The Public's Interest." *Communications and the Law.* 4:2, Winter 1982. pp.51-58.

CHAPTER II

THE FCC AND THE FAIRNESS DOCTRINE, 1969-1980

Although the focus of this study is to develop an historical chronology of the FCC's activity between 1981 and 1987, an understanding of the situation existing prior to this period is also necessary. This chapter is to provide such historical context, and is necessary for three important reasons. First, it is necessary to understand how the application of the fairness doctrine had evolved during the period between the 1969 *Red Lion*[1] decision, and the arrival of Mark Fowler as chairman of the commission in 1981. Second, it is important to understand that communications deregulation, which was the guiding principle of both Mark Fowler's and Dennis Patrick's FCC, did not originate with them. Instead, communications deregulation began under the Democratic chairmanship of Charles Ferris during the late 1970's. But what the term communications deregulation meant differed markedly between Ferris and Fowler. And how these meanings changed require first understanding communications deregulation's original conceptualization. Third, an understanding of the negative relationship chairman Ferris had with both the broadcast industry and Congress is also essential. Understanding this negative relationship helps provide needed context for Fowler's arrival in 1981.

Beyond the 1969 Red Lion Decision

Discussion of what the fairness doctrine *means* predates the Fowler FCC. The doctrine was originally conceived by the FCC as a narrowly tailored means of providing the most basic audience access to a diversity of ideas. But as the limits of the doctrine's power was tested, commercial broadcasters became increasingly concerned. As mentioned earlier, the strongest affirmation for the doctrine's appropriateness came in 1969 when the U.S. Supreme Court unanimously upheld its constitutionality in *Red Lion*. This affirmation did not end the controversy though. It simply clarified some of the rules of the game.

An example of testing the doctrine's limits can be seen as early as 1970. Then the United States Court of Appeals, District of Columbia, suggested that the FCC should look deeper into whether the fairness doctrine should be extended to cover advertising in any way judged controversial.[2] Not surprisingly, public interest groups argued the doctrine did extend to advertising. But broadcasters just as strongly argued the doctrine was never intended to cover advertising. Advertising, being at the core of the U.S. commercial broadcast system, was interestingly to provide the test of the doctrine's continued existence in the 1980's. As represented in a 1971 FCC Fairness Doctrine Inquiry,[3] commercial broadcasters were concerned that any advertising involving an issue that met the controversial test could trigger the fairness doctrine and force an accommodation on them of messages to counteract the advertising. Their fear was not simply loss of editorial control, but also the fear of lost revenue. Although these fears of economic loss were quickly subsumed by higher moral arguments, such as a loss of editorial discretion, the economic issues were never far below the surface.

On June 21, 1971, Richard W. Jencks, president of CBS/Broadcast Group characterized the situation over the growing issue of citizen access as a fear that stations could be turned into common carriers if outsiders (read the public) continued to be appeased in their demands for time.[4] The FCC sought to address these concerns in 1971, when it opened a docket re-examining the fairness doctrine.[5] It concluded this inquiry in 1974 when it issued a Fairness Report.[6] The commission concluded the fairness doctrine imposed a minimum obligation on broadcasters, and there was no danger of broadcasters being turned into common carriers.

Broadcasters did not accept the commission's decision without question. For example, even while the commission's docket was open, some 50 academicians, lawyers and broadcast and print journalists, met in Cambridge, Mass., on June 8-9, 1973. There they approved recommendations calling for essentially the same freedom for broadcasters that the print media enjoyed.[7] Including no fairness doctrine. This document came to be called the Warren Conference Report.

The conference came about as a backlash on the part of commercial broadcasters. They were rallying against what they saw as a growing effort on the part of the courts and public-interest groups to restrict their discretion (both editorial and economic). To strengthen their argument, they drew on a decision handed down just three weeks prior to this meeting. The U.S. Supreme Court in *CBS v. DNC*[8] upheld the right of broadcasters to impose a flat ban on editorial advertising. The final recommendations drew heavily on a separate opinion written by Justice William O. Douglas in this case. Douglas categorically held that broadcasters were entitled to the same first amendment rights as newspapers. The recommendations contained in the Warren Conference report asserted that the marketplace, including a station's ratings and its concerns with its public image, provided adequate control of broadcasting.[9]

There is good reason for devoting more focus to the Warren Conference report here rather than the FCC's own 1974 Fairness Report. Because the Fowler commission's 1985 Fairness Doctrine report drew much more on the rationale of the Warren Conference than it did on the commission's own 1974 report rationale.

1978-1981

With the arrival of Charles Ferris as FCC chairman in 1978 communications deregulation began in earnest. But broadcasters were at best skeptical of Ferris. And at times they were even hostile. Ferris' six stated goals as chairman were:

(1) Establish an office of chief economist to let the Commission know the impact of its decisions on the economy;

(2) Consider a rule to make radio and TV licensees divulge their profits;

(3) Start a major study of the broadcast networks, which are not now licensed, to see how they affect local stations and society in general;

(4) Find ways to speed up the agency's adjudicatory process;

(5) Investigate whether broadcasters do an adequate job of self-policing in children's programming; and

(6) Expand the Commission's capacity to make long-range forecasts of new trends.[10]

These goals showed little deference to broadcasters. The most notable effect that Ferris had on the FCC was shifting its focus. Prior to Ferris, the commission acted on primarily technical and legal grounds. But Ferris believed the commission should also focus on economic impacts. And it was this shift in focus to economic impacts that drove both the Fowler and the Patrick commissions in the 1980's. The difference between Ferris' focus on economic and impacts and Fowler's are worth noting though. Ferris established an economic office to study the effects on the economy. Fowler used the economic office to show the economic effects on broadcasters.

Also in 1978, Congress began considering legislation to re-write the Communications Act of 1934.[11] This began first with a Communications Subcommittee consideration of a Staff Report.[12] Although discussions of this staff report broke down quickly, it served as the first in a series of Communications Act re-write considerations. All of these re-write attempts failed, but the discussions they generated illustrate Congressional inability to agree on its own wishes. Congress has ultimate responsibility for setting the direction of communications policy, but their inability to lead in this area was to have a major impact in the 1980's.

A second re-write bill (HR-13015 or "Re-write II") was introduced June 7, 1978, and its cornerstone was a spectrum fee, or broadcast license fee. The spectrum fee would produce in excess of $250 million a year to pay the bills of what was envisioned as the FCC successor, the Communications Regulatory Commission.[13] But it too became mired in the political process and died.

In 1978 the commission also initiated another inquiry into its administration of the fairness doctrine. This inquiry asked for comments on two proposals. First, it sought comments on establishing a system of voluntary access. Second, it sought comments on requiring licensees to cover a specified number of controversial issues of public importance. Both ideas had been rejected by the commission in 1974. But both were sent back to the commission by the courts for reconsideration. Comments filed for this 1978 inquiry by broadcasters spoke against both ideas, while consumer groups generally favored them.[14]

Also, the commission in June 1978, revived its investigation into network practices.[15] The National Association of Broadcasters (NAB) took advantage of this opportunity to restate its opposition to what it called broadcasters' "second class citizenship" with regard to first amendment guarantees. As it had done previously, the NAB called the fairness doctrine "unconstitutional" and "wholly unnecessary."[16]

The third proposed re-write of the 1934 Communications Act ("Re-write III") was introduced in January 1979 (HR-3333). Provisions of this re-write contained:

(1) a license fee for broadcasters;

(2) extension of the broadcast license term longer than the current three years;

(3) retained the fairness doctrine and equal time provisions; and

(4) provided for federal regulation of cable but with relaxed signal carriage rules.[17]

Like the two preceding attempts, this proposed re-write also failed. HR-3333 focused on a means of "quantifying" the public-trustee responsibility of television licensees. House subcommittee Democrats wanted to maintain the public trustee concept. They claimed it was this obligation that required broadcasters to operate in the public interest. They feared if the public trustee concept was removed, it could not be recovered if competition failed to protect the public interest. Ferris also urged retaining the public interest standard. He referred to it as a "safety net."[18]

Much like media coverage of the debate of the fairness doctrine in the 1980's, this bill was given limited public exposure. Even though this legislation contained policy provisions that would affect technological innovation and industry structures in communications well into the next century, little national and local news coverage was provided. There was no coverage of the hearings on these bills, and little interest by the news media to publicize the frustration and anger of public-interest groups.[19]

In January 1979, Senator Proxmire reintroduced his bill to abolish the fairness doctrine and equal time. Like the original version introduced in the 94th Congress, the bill also died in committee.[20]

1979 also saw Ferris' commission begin to focus on controlling broadcasters structure rather than their behavior. In many ways this signalled the real beginning of deregulation. Ferris believed this "structural" approach could "substantially increase the likelihood of diversity in programing" while posing fewer first amendment problems.[21]

What were these "structural" rather than "behavioral" regulations that appeared essential to Ferris? They included the use of antitrust policies, media-crossownership limitations, and the imposition of access requirement on cable systems. Ferris believed "structural" regulation would "permit rectifying undesirable aspects of the market without government involvement in program content."[22]

Ferris, not Fowler, was also the first to say, "the public interest can most effectively be voiced by the public itself as it turns the dials of television sets across the country to choose among an abundance of program choices."[23] But, unlike Fowler, Ferris believed the FCC's primary responsibility was fulfilling the Congressional mandate of serving the interest of the public.

But Ferris was not fully supported by his own commission. FCC commissioner James H. Quello, for example, told the nation's independent broadcasters (Association of Independent Television Stations) in February, 1979, that the time had come to "emancipate broadcasters from all First Amendment restraints."[24]

But the commission was not yet ready to act on its own. For example, Republican commission nominee Anne Jones, in her February 23, 1979, nomination hearing, said that "only Congress can relieve the broadcaster of its public trustee obligation."[25] She also said she believed there was ample room for the commission to reexamine rules which it had adopted to be sure they were still necessary and appropriate to fulfill its Congressional mandate. Jones said that if intervening experience and changes in industry practice or technology made such rules no longer necessary, such rules might properly be rescinded or modified.[26]

When Jones was asked whether Section 315 of the Act could be repealed, she replied that repeal of Section 315 "is entirely up to Congress."[27] When asked specifically about the fairness doctrine she replied:

> The fairness doctrine ... is presently the law and I would expect it to be conscientiously and faithfully implemented by the Commission in its current and future broadcast regulation unless and until it is modified or repealed. I am aware of arguments which are gaining wider currency that the doctrine, though well intentioned, may inhibit free speech on the airways. Any alternative must be very carefully weighed and the intimate relationship between it and the First

Amendment make this an area in which a regulator must exercise extreme caution. Access to the media for persons with contrasting views on controversial issues is an important social goal, but the journalistic discretion of the broadcast media is no less deserving of protection under the First Amendment from governmental intrusion than is that of the print media. The Commission must exercise whatever authority it has in this area with special sensitivity to any potentially "chilling" inferences to be drawn from its actions.[28]

Unlike Jones, Democratic commissioner Tyrone Brown's June 29, 1979, renomination hearing contained no questions about the fairness doctrine. They were not necessary because of his longstanding support of the doctrine. As to Brown's feeling about the trustee model of regulation, Charles Ferris said this of Brown:

> I know of no one that I have served with in public life that has a greater sense of the public interest and the meaning of the public trustee obligation than Tyrone Brown.[29]

Deregulation was the buzzword of both the Carter administration and the Ferris commission. But the Carter administration remained committed to "pursuing the legitimate goals of regulation in ways that are rational, predictable and effective."[30]   Carter's proposal for broadcast deregulation, as he presented them at the 1979 NAB convention, had five major goals:

> (1) to assure that costs and benefits of all major regulations and rules are weighed before they are issued;
>
> (2) to help reduce the enormous inventory of rules and regulations that have accumulated over the years even though they have long since outlived their usefulness;
>
> (3) to put a brake on the regulatory assembly line;
>
> (4) to end needless delays and endless procedural nightmares; and
>
> (5) to open up the rulemaking process to all Americans ... not just the best-financed and best-organized interest groups.[31]

This last goal did not set well with broadcasters.

One of Ferris' more controversial appointments to further his goal of deregulation was naming Philip Verveer, who had been head of the Cable Bureau for 14 months, as chief of the Broadcast Bureau on May 2, 1979.[32] There had been opposition to the selection of Mr. Verveer both from within the commission and from the broadcast industry. One unnamed NAB executive was quoted as saying that, with Mr.

Verveer as chief of the Broadcast Bureau, broadcasters are "like a hockey team without a goalie in the net."[33]   Verveer shared much of Ferris' enthusiasm for deregulation.   But, also like Ferris, Verveer believed current conditions warranted continued protection of the rights of the public.[34]

On May 8, 1979, the FCC announced its intention to deregulate the nation's 8,400 radio stations.[35]   On the basis of staff reports of the Plans and Policy Office, FCC Chairman Charles Ferris said that a case had been made for "the uselessness of our rules."   FCC economists had determined there was no need for radio stations to adhere to regulations that required a minimum of broadcast time (8 percent) be set aside by AM stations for news and other nonentertainment programming.[36]   But the Carter Administration was not ready to remove all rules from radio and television.

As Carter's term ended, growing dissent within the FCC also surfaced.   This dissent concerned both the administration and the policies of Chairman Ferris.   This internal dissent was given wide coverage in *Broadcasting* magazine.   This was not surprising, given the fact its editors had long been opposed to Ferris.[37]

The General Accounting Office (GAO) also released a report in 1979 criticizing management at almost every level of the FCC.[38]   This report was referenced often during Mark Fowler's nomination hearing, and *Broadcasting* also gave it extensive coverage as if to illustrate its gripes with the Ferris commission.   Ferris responded to this GAO report in several ways.   One particular maneuver was a major reorganization of the Broadcast Bureau.[39]

At a November, 1979, FCC oversight hearing the broadcast networks provided its views on a number of issues.   These included mandatory access, the fairness doctrine, the media coverage of itself, and the GAO's assessment of the commission.   This testimony provides a glimpse of the issues that characterized the 1980's.   Everett Erlick, senior vice president and general counsel of ABC, claimed that if mandatory public access were instituted as a substitute for the fairness doctrine, the public agenda "would be set by a few vocal partisans for particular causes or by those who could buy time to air their editorial views."[40]   Corydon Dunham, executive vice president and general counsel for NBC, called the fairness doctrine "an aberration," that should be abolished.[41]

Speaking to the issue of the media's coverage of itself, Andrew Schwartzman, director of the public interest organization, Media Access Project (MAP), complained about the lack of networks' coverage of themselves. He added that the networks have adopted "a reprehensible position" concerning the presentation of viewpoints on controversial issues. "The arrogant assumption that Mobil and Ralph Nader cannot present their opinions forcefully, while Eric Sevareid can, deprives the listeners of the chance to make first-hand judgments about these issues."[42]

As to the GAO's assessment of the FCC's effectiveness, Henry Eschwege, a GAO official, told the subcommittee that the chairman's role should be strengthened. Another flaw of the agency, Eschwege said, was that it lacked comprehensive future and short-term plans.[43]

Though a complete legislative revision of the Communications Act of 1934 fizzled, deregulation as a goal survived. But the focus moved from Congress to the FCC. The Fowler commission, without explicit Congressional directive, decided to reinterpret existing law with regard to broadcasting.[44] It also was to reinterpret the meaning of deregulation.

Notes

[1]*Red Lion Broadcasting Co. v. Federal Communications Commission*, 395 U.S. 361 (1969).

[2]*Friends of the Earth*, 24 FCC 2d 743 (1970), rev'd, 449 F.2d 1164 (D.C. Cir. 1971).
    In 1967, the commission had ruled that the advertisement of cigarettes raised a controversial issue of public importance and thus applied the doctrine to product advertising for the first time. See WCBS-TV, 8 FCC 2d 381, stay and recon. denied, 9 FCC 2d 921 (1967), aff'd, *Banzhaf v. FCC*. 405 F.2d 1082 (1968), cert. denied, 396 U.S. 842 (1969).

[3]The Handling of Public Issues Under the Fairness Doctrine and the Public Interest Standards of the Communications Act. Notice of Inquiry. 30 FCC 2d 26 (1971).

[4]"On the unfairness of fairness." *Broadcasting*. June 21, 1971. p.88.

[5]The Handling of Public Issues Under the Fairness Doctrine and the Public Interest Standards of the Communications Act. Notice of Inquiry. 30 FCC 2d 26 (1971).

[6]*Fairness Report* in Docket No. 19260, 48 FCC 2d 1 (1974), recon. denied, 58 FCC 2d 691 (1976), aff'd sub nom. *National Citizens Committee for Broadcasting v. FCC*, 567 F.2d 1095 (D.C. Cir. 1977), cert. denied, 436 U.S. 926 (1978) ["*1974 Fairness Report*"].

[7]"A strong vote for de-regulation." *Broadcasting*. June 18, 1973. pp.35-6.

[8]*Columbia Broadcasting System, Inc v. Democratic National Committee*, 412 U.S. 94 (1973).

[9]*Broadcasting*, June 18, 1973.

[10]"New chairman outlines his plans: Charles Ferris intends to streamline commission." *U.S. News & World Report*. v.84. January 30, 1978. p.40.

[11]See: "The rise and fall of the third rewrite." Manny Lucoff. *Journal of Broadcasting*. Summer 1980.

[12]U.S. House, Committee on Interstate and Foreign Commerce, Communications Subcommittee, 95th Congress, 1st Session, *Options Papers* (Staff Report), May 1977.

[13]"The year that was: Looking to the years that will be." *Broadcasting*. January 1, 1979. pp.56-62. At p.56.

[14]Ibid., at p.58.

[15]See: Network Inquiry Special Staff: A Review of the Proceedings of the FCC Leading to the Adoption of the Prime Time Access Rule, the Financial Interest Rule, and the Syndication Rule. FCC. October 1979; and Network Inquiry Special Staff: Preliminary Report on Prospects for Additional Networks. FCC. February 1980.

[16]"Fairness policy rulemaking draws different opinions." *Broadcasting*. January 1, 1979. p.66.

[17]"New Congress convenes with more-than-usual number of matters for broadcasting." *Broadcasting*. January 15, 1979. p.34.

[18]"Ready to rewrite the rewrite." *Broadcasting*. 97:1. July 2, 1979. pp.31-2. At p.31.

[19]"Potomac fever: Deregulating telecommunications." Donald C. Matthews. *America*. v.141. July 7, 1979. pp.6-8. At p.8.

[20]"The new Congress: Legislative reruns and few new faces." *Broadcasting*. January 22, 1979. p.30.

[21]"Bazelon, Ferris: More sources of programs mean less regulation." *Broadcasting*. 96:6. February 5, 1979. pp.29-30. At p.29.

[22]Ibid.

[23]Ibid., at p.30.

[24]"First Amendment pep talk from FCC's Quello." *Broadcasting*. v.96. February 12, 1979. p.39.

[25]Nominations to the Federal Communications Commission: Nomination of Anne P. Jones. February 23, 1979. Serial No. 96-40. At p.2.

[26]Ibid.

[27]Ibid., at p.3.

[28]Ibid.

[29]Nominations to the Federal Communications Commission: Nomination of Tyrone Brown, June 28, 1979. Serial No. 96-46. At p.7.

[30]"Carter's pledge of deregulation to NAB falls on welcome ears." *Broadcasting*. v.96. April 2, 1979. pp.38,41. At p.38.

[31]Ibid.

[32]"Broadcast Bureau job goes to Verveer, but not without a struggle." *Broadcasting*. v.96. May 7, 1979. pp.33,35. At p.33.

[33]Ibid.

[34]"A deregulator's regulator." *Broadcasting*. v.96. May 14, 1979. pp.32,34. At p.32.

[35]Inquiry and Notice of Proposed Rule Making in BC Docket No. 79-219, 73 FCC 2d 457 (1979); Report and Order in BC Docket No. 79-219, 84 FCC 2d 968 (1981), recon. denied, 87 FCC 2d 797 (1981), rev'd on other grounds sub nom. *United Church of Christ v. FCC*, 707 F.2d 1413 (D.C. Cir. 1973).

[36]"Potomac fever: Deregulating telecommunications." Donald C. Matthews. *America*. v.141. July 7, 1979. pp.6-8. At p.8.

[37]"At the FCC: Heat's on high." *Broadcasting*. 97:7. August 13, 1979. pp.21,23.

[38]"Shiben's shop to be restructured." *Broadcasting*. v.97. November 12, 1979. p.61.

[39]Ibid.

[40]"Weapons are put away for FCC oversight hearings on Hill." *Broadcasting*. 97:21. November 19, 1979. pp.28-32. At p.31.

[41]Ibid.

[42]Ibid.

[43]Ibid.

[44]"Freedom from restraints." *America*. February 2, 1980. v.142. p.70.

CHAPTER III

THE FEDERAL COMMUNICATIONS COMMISSION AND THE FAIRNESS DOCTRINE, 1981-83

1981: The Period from Ronald Reagan's Election through Mark Fowler's First Year as FCC Chairman

As indicated above, the fairness doctrine required licensees to provide reasonable opportunity for opposing sides to debate controversial issues on the air. The FCC does not tell licensees what programs they should run, or precisely when they should run them. As Milton Gross, chief of fairness enforcement for the FCC explained it in 1981, "the fairness doctrine has room for interpretation by individual licensees. If they want to give equal time for response to a controversial issue, they can. But they don't have to."[1] This was the agency's view in early 1981.

With Ronald Reagan in the White House, Washington's vast rule-making machine was to come in for extensive overhaul. Less than a week after the election, Murray Weidenbaum, chief of the President-elect's regulatory task force, called for a freeze on new government rules during the first year of the new administration.[2] Reagan advisers vowed that the new heads of regulatory agencies would be under more pressure than ever to justify the costs of new standards versus the benefits they sought to achieve.[3]

Reagan had the opportunity to put his stamp on the FCC early in his administration by naming a successor to Charles Ferris. And before the end of 1982, Reagan would also be able to name two more commission members. The focus of Reagan's regulators was to be on the "bottom line"--does a new rule's benefits outweigh its costs.[4]

Charles Ferris had a reputation for being more of a Republican than a Republican might have been. Ferris' conservative reputation notwithstanding, it is also necessary to recognize his unpopularity with broadcasters. He seldom deferred to their wishes. And with such Ferris statements as "there had been a subtle capture of the agency by the companies in those industries,"[5] it is not difficult to understand broadcaster concern. Ferris was credited with moving the agency from one dominated by lawyers to one influenced heavily by economists. As he represented it, "we're an economic regulatory agency ... so I more than doubled the number of economists, to about 100."[6]

But Ferris was now out, and the White House transition team announced that Robert Lee would serve as interim chairman of the FCC. As early as January, 1981, Mark Fowler was the "odds-on" favorite to be appointed FCC chairman.[7] Fowler was a partner in the Washington law firm Fowler & Meyers, and had formerly been with Smith & Pepper. He had worked for Reagan in his campaign, and had prepared answers for Reagan to questions submitted by the NAB to Presidential candidates. He was 39 years old, a graduate of University of Florida Law School, and a strong advocate of deregulation.[8]

In line for the second Republican vacancy at the FCC was Mary Ann (Mimi) Weyforth, administrative assistant to Senator Packwood (R-Oregon). With Republicans capturing the majority in the Senate, Packwood was the new chairman of the Senate Commerce Committee. Weyforth was 36 years old, a graduate of Washington University (St. Louis) and St. Louis University law school. She had started on the Hill in 1968 as legislative assistant to ex-Senator Symington (D-Missouri), and joined Packwood in 1972.[9]

FCC commissioner Tyrone Brown, whose term would have expired in 1984, announced his resignation in January. He had hoped for the chairmanship with a Democratic victory, but with Reagan's victory Brown decided to move back into the private sector.[10]

In the last week of February, Reagan introduced a major tax and budget cut package. His economic package was driven by the concept of deregulation. Reagan was also appointing new agency heads who shared his views. He also expected them to slash the budgets of their agencies.[11] Reagan's budget chief, David Stockman, called the regulatory process a "ticking regulatory time bomb." Stockman's rhetoric was apocalyptic. "Unless something is done," Stockman warned the President, the mass of regulations "would sweep through the industrial economy with near-gale force, pre-empting [sic] billions in investment capital, driving up operating costs and siphoning off management and technical personnel in an incredible morass of new controls and compliance procedures."[12] Vice President Bush was appointed head of a cabinet-level Task Force on Regulatory Relief. The task force was established with the intent to enforce a new Executive Order that required regulatory agencies to determine the economic impact of any proposed regulation, and pursue only those rules whose benefits outweigh their costs.[13]

Reagan asserted that what he could not do by fiat or legislation he would try to accomplish by appointing sympathetic administrators.[14] To win Congressional support for his programs, Reagan counted on a current, popular anti-government sentiment. And he dispatched Bush, a former congressman, to lobby for Congressional reform.[15]

Friday, March 6, the White House announced the nomination of Mark Fowler as FCC chairman. Fowler was nominated to fill the unexpired seven year term of commissioner Quello's from July 1, 1979. It was expected Quello would be nominated for the seat vacated by the resignation of Tyrone Brown.[16]

Fowler had specialized in representing radio, television, domestic and private radio stations throughout the United States before the FCC. He had been a guest speaker over the past 5 years at more than 20 conventions sponsored by the NAB and various state broadcasters associations.[17] He also had served as FCC communications counsel to Citizens for Reagan in 1975-76 and to the Reagan for President Committee in 1979-80.

Broadcast industry reaction to Fowler's nomination was swift and positive. For instance, John Summers, NAB executive vice-president and general manager, said of Fowler, "as a practicing communications attorney, I know he's been close to the nitty gritty of broadcasting. He has a better understanding [than commissioner Ferris] and appreciation of the functions of broadcasting in the local community."[18]

Speculation about Fowler's staff appointments began immediately, with much focus centered on his choice of FCC general counsel. Most believed he would choose Stephen Sharp who was a former member of the general counsel's staff, and legal aide to ex-commissioner White.

Sharp was currently with the Washington office of Philadelphia law firm Schnader, Harrison, Segal & Lewis.[19]

Pending Fowler's expected approval by the Senate, commissioner Robert Lee was appointed acting chairman. Speaking providentially at a Federal Communications Bar Association luncheon in New York City, Lee said deregulation was a "buzz word" used by regulators and those regulated, "but no one who is regulated or who benefits from the regulation wants the full impact of increased competition and decreased protection or decreased benefits which may flow from deregulation."[20]

President Reagan announced on Monday, April 6, 1981, his intention to nominate Mary Ann Weyforth Dawson to be an FCC commissioner. She was nominated for a term of 7 years from July 1, 1981. She would replace acting chairman Robert E. Lee, whose term was to expire on June 30, 1981. Dawson at that time was serving as press secretary to Senator Robert Packwood (R-Oregon).[21]

Speculation on who would be named to fill the traditional "minority" seat vacated by the resignation of Tyrone Brown was also a hot topic. Albuquerque lawyer Henry Rivera, 34, was considered the top contender.[22] If nominated, Rivera would be the first Hispanic at the FCC. He was a Democrat, and a partner in the firm of Sutin, Thayer & Brown. He was president-elect of Albuquerque Bar Association and one of the youngest persons nominated to commission.

Fowler's nomination hearing before the Senate was held on Friday, May 1, 1981. There were obvious partisan differences regarding the performance of Fowler's predecessor Charles Ferris, as well as the future role of the FCC. As Republican Senator Barry Goldwater said:[23]

> As you probably know, I urged President Reagan to make Charlie Ferris' removal a matter of the highest priority.
>
> I am convinced that much of what the FCC has done in the past will be irrelevant in the future. ... Marketplace competition will guarantee the delivery of these service, not pervasive Government regulation.

Particularly fortuitous was Goldwater's statement:

> And I want to stress that Congress will establish the telecommunications policy, not the Commission or the courts.[24]

This part of Goldwater's statement may not have borne out, but the next part certainly did:

> The bottom line is that you are going to be seeing and hearing from us much more often than the Commission has in the past.[25]

Fowler's background gave many clues as to what to expect of his chairmanship. First was his work as legal counsel for the Virginia Association of Broadcasters from 1979 to 1981. Unlike Ferris, Fowler's links to broadcasting were sound. He had been named Virginian of the Year in 1981 by the Virginia Association of Broadcasters. Another element of Fowler's background which was to play a significant role during his tenure as chairman was his penchant for public speaking. Fowler listed on his vita that he had received Best Individual Debater honors from the National Forensic League in an 1959 Florida High School State Competition, and he had won Best Oral Argument in a Moot Court Competition at the University of Florida College of Law in 1967. During his time as chairman he was credited with using his bully pulpit for nearly 200 public addresses.[26]

Fowler's own testimony provided a glimpse of his ideas for the agency. Fowler said his philosophy emphasized "consumer choice and entrepreneurial initiative over pervasive Government control and direction."[27] He claimed that "in implementing this philosophy, I am committed to creating an atmosphere of constructive cooperation with, and respect for the public, and the regulated industry, and to avoid a regulatory climate of rancor, deception or mutual mistrust.[28] But implementation of this philosophy was to prove more beneficial for the regulated industries than to the general public.

When asked by Goldwater if he supported Congressional oversight of the commission, Fowler responded "I not only support it but I welcome working with the Congress in partnership.[29]

When Senator Cannon asked Fowler how he felt about three-year agency authorizations rather than on-going authorizations, Fowler responded:

> I would not necessarily oppose a 3-year authorization (S. 821). At the same time I would ask the Congress to remain sensitive to the fact that this particular agency does administer Section 315 political equal time provisions and Section 312 reasonable political access. And it might be that members of Congress would have ongoing cases before the agency at the time that the basic agency authorization is up for

renewal. I think it is just something that the Congress ought to be sensitive to, but, no, I would not oppose a 3-year authorization.[30]

Interestingly absent in Fowler's confirmation hearing was any questioning, especially by Democrats, of his views on the fairness doctrine. Though he had been an vocal opponent of it for years, it is curious that there was no questioning of this during his confirmation.

On the same day as Fowler's confirmation hearing the Senate also held an FCC authorization hearing. Testimony was provided by Henry Eschwege, Director of Community and Economic Development Division, General Accounting Office.[31] Eschwege, quoted from the July 1979 GAO report mentioned earlier, titled "Organizing the Federal Communications Commission for Greater Management and Regulatory Effectiveness." Eschwege cited several key recommendations from the report. Particularly, that the GAO recommended the desirability of maintaining close congressional scrutiny and oversight of the commission's operation. The GAO believed such oversight should increase commission accountability; provide it with increased congressional guidance; and keep the Congress better informed of developments and activities at the commission, as well as in the field of communications generally.[32]

The GAO believed that legislation setting program objectives and evaluating program performance at the FCC were two critical elements needed for an effective review process.[33] The GAO also recommended that the commission's decision-making and its overall effectiveness would be improved by modifying the commission's size, composition and structure. Specifically, the GAO favored: (1) reducing the number of commissioners from seven to five; (2) strengthening the chairman's role as administrative head of the agency; (3) providing for Senate confirmation of the chairman; (4) legislatively establishing the position of managing director at the commission; and, (5) lengthening the terms of the commissioners.[34]

As it turned out Congress would act selectively on these recommendations. And politics, more than logic, would figure highly into the final implementation of these recommendations.

On May 21st the Senate held a nomination hearing for Republican commission nominee, Mary Ann Weyforth Dawson. Here she described her philosophy:

> Like President Reagan, I believe we need to encourage the proper function of market forces by eliminating unnecessary regulation.[35]

She also endorsed the Senate Committee's recommendation calling for new management procedures at the commission. When asked by Senator Goldwater for her views on radio deregulation, she stated she believed "there have been a lot of unnecessary requirements in radio broadcasting," and she supported legislation to help "free up the marketplace."[36]

As to her views on television deregulation, she said she was very much in favor of legislation to provide for greater competition and an "unburdening of the industry."[37] Just as with Fowler's nomination hearing, it is curious that no questions were raised by Democratic members as to Dawson's views on the fairness doctrine.

In May, 1981 the commissioners, their party affiliation, their terms of office, and who they had been appointed by looked like this:

Mark S. Fowler,		
Chairman Designate (R)	June 1988	Reagan
Mimi Weyforth Dawson (R)	June 1988	Reagan
Robert E. Lee (R)	Oct. 1981	Nixon
Joseph Fogarty (D)	June 1983	Ford
Anne Jones (R)	June 1986	Carter
James Quello (D)	Oct. 1980	Nixon
Abbot Washburn (R)	Oct. 1982	Ford
One Vacancy		

So, as of May, Reagan still had two out of seven commission slots to fill, and by the middle of 1982, he would have the opportunity to fill five of the seven. Reagan had an unprecedented opportunity to set the direction of the commission.

Under former Democratic chairman, Charles Ferris, the FCC had moved to deregulate the cable TV, radio, and the telecommunications industries. That had delighted the cable companies, which grew exponentially. This concerned broadcasters, though, particularly network executives. They just were not used to the competition.[38]

Fowler's appointment particularly pleased broadcasters. They felt that Ferris was moving much too fast on the deregulatory front, and was doing so at their expense. This was especially at the cost of forcing competition on them. John Summers, executive vice president of NAB, said "we like Fowler because we believe he has a good feel for the nitty-gritty of broadcasting."[39]

Mark Fowler was sworn in as the nineteenth FCC chairman on Tuesday, May 19, 1981. He promised he would be "guided by one question and one question alone: What is best for the people."[40] At that time he also announced some of his personal staff. These included Willard Nichols, administrative assistant; Lauren Belvin, legal assistant; Jerald Fritz and Edward Minkel, special assistants. Other Fowler appointments included Stephen Sharp, as general counsel, and acting general counsel Marjorie Reed moved to deputy general counsel. And Peter Pitsch, general regulatory attorney with Montgomery Ward's Washington legal office, would head the Office of Plans & Policy.[41]

At his swearing in Fowler provided a list of five objectives he had as chairman:

(1) To create, to the maximum extent possible, an unregulated, competitive marketplace environment for the development of telecommunications;

(2) To eliminate unnecessary regulation and policies;

(3) To provide service to the public in the most efficient, expeditious manner possible;

(4) To promote the coordination and planning of international communications which assures the vital interests of the American public in commerce, defense and foreign policy;

(5) To eliminate government action that infringes the freedom of speech and the press.[42]

His pursuit of the fifth objective provides most of the focus here.

Early on, it was believed Fowler would work closely with Congress. This made Congress particularly happy because they felt that Ferris' "structural" deregulation ignored Congress. And Congress was now interested in reasserting its authority over communications policy and the agency.[43]

So Fowler started off well. He had both the support of Congress, and the industry he was to regulate. Broadcasters believed that, once again, "they had a friend in the FCC."[44] Fowler clearly was sympathetic to broadcast interest. For example, one bane to broadcasters pursued by Ferris was a plan to reduce the spacing between AM radio stations from 10 kilohertz to 9 kilohertz. This would had added approximately 1,000 new stations to the U.S. airwaves. Broadcasters had ardently opposed this change. Even though there were competitive issues involved, they argued against it on technical grounds. So when Fowler announced that he had "grave reservations about the engineering behind this proposal," Fowler was showing his deference to the broadcasters. This was particularly evident when he continued by saying "I'll look to the industry for help with it."[45]

President Reagan, on Friday, June 5, 1981, announced his nomination of Henry M. Rivera to be a member of the FCC for the term expiring June 30, 1987.[46] Reagan, at the same time, announced the renomination of James Quello to be a member of the FCC for the remainder of the term of Charles Ferris expiring June 30, 1984.[47] Quello, a Democrat, had been a member of the FCC since 1974. From 1972 to 1974, Quello was a communications consultant in Michigan, and from 1947 to 1972, he was vice president and station manager for Goodwill Stations, Inc., in Detroit, Michigan.[48]

This was Fowler's honeymoon period. At a July 23, 1981, oversight hearing before the House Telecommunications Subcommittee, Fowler, in a prepared statement told the Subcommittee that the FCC could not "fully accomplish" its regulatory objectives in some areas without legislation. He promised to send his recommendations to Congress in the fall. There was already heavy speculation that these recommendations include abolition of the fairness doctrine.[49] Fowler also told the Subcommittee that starting in the fall there would be regular commission meetings 2-3 days a week.[50]

Confirmation hearings for Democratic nominees James Quello and Henry Rivera were held on Wednesday, July 22nd. Quello, a former newscaster and broadcast executive himself, said at the hearing, that one of the most important issues for him was first amendment rights.[51] Quello told the Senate Commerce Committee that he believed full first amendment rights had been withheld from the electronic media. But, he said, he realized that "key changes in the Communications Act are the prerogatives of Congress, not the FCC," and continued that "the time may be propitious for Congress to review the first amendment rights in view of the current communications explosion."[52]

This stand, especially for a Democrat, was not as difficult to understand as may be thought. Quello was a member of the NAB and from 1963 to 1972, served on the NAB Congressional Liaison Committee, and from 1966 to 1971 on its National Radio Code

Board.[53] In an addendum statement to his nomination hearing, Quello added:

> I propose clean, decisive, legislative surgery to remove the major pervasive defects and massive economic wastes of broadcast regulation.   Unequivocally remove all First Amendment and regulatory constraints!   Subject broadcasting to exactly the same regulations and First Amendment constraints as its major competitor and closest cousin--newspapers.   This also means eliminating the nebulous, troublesome and out-dated "public interest" standard.[54]

By 1987 he would change his mind on the lack of utility of the public interest standard. Further on in this addendum Quello added:

> I believe the public would be served by abolishing Section 315 including the Fairness Doctrine and Section 312(1)(7). The Fairness Doctrine is a codification of good journalistic practice. Its goals are laudatory. However, I no longer believe government is the proper source for mandating good journalistic or program practice. I believe the practice of journalism is better governed by professional journalists, editors and news directors.[55]

Henry Rivera differed from Quello in his understanding of the desirability of the abolition of the fairness doctrine. His approach was much more cautious. His uncertainty was indicated in the following exchange with Senator Schmitt:

> Senator Schmitt: Mr. Rivera, do you care to comment on this first amendment issue? It is something that the Congress has danced around for some time, but one which I think is going to have to be visited.

> Mr. Rivera: I really haven't had an opportunity to study that. I think that the Supreme Court has indicated that broadcasters do have less first amendment rights than other types of journalists. And I support first amendment rights for broadcasters.

> But the issues involved are terribly complex. As with most policy issues, one is not always going to make everyone happy, and I think it is something that I would need to study in great depth.[56]

At a radio programming conference of the NAB in Chicago during the third week of August, Mark Fowler stated, as he would continue to do during his entire tenure, that the FCC had "encroached upon freedom of speech in many areas." He promised that this would not happen during his administration.[57] Explaining President Reagan's philosophy, as it applied to broadcasting, Fowler stressed that this philosophy was to let broadcasters do what they do best without government interference.[58]

Fowler said the commission would rely on the public interest in its efforts to deregulate. He promised he would say next month how the Reagan Administration defined the public interest in broadcasting.[59] Commissioner Quello, speaking at the same NAB conference, also urged broadcasters to take advantage of the current Washington trends and push hard for full first amendment rights from the commission and Congress.[60]

Later the same week Henry Rivera was sworn in in Albuquerque, New Mexico. Speaking at Rivera's ceremony, Fowler said the goals of the Reagan Administration were to "promote an unregulated and competitive marketplace, provide faster service to licensees and public, protect U.S. interests in international communications and eliminate government infringements on the First Amendment."[61]

In a move called "revolutionary" by the commissioners, the FCC in the third week of September proposed that Congress give major new freedoms to broadcasters.[62] The commission's wish list included asking Congress to repeal fairness doctrine, equal time and reasonable access provisions and personal attack rule.[63] Its recommendations provoked a demonstration outside FCC headquarters. And commissioner James Fogarty in his dissent to these recommendations said that "with this action, we've become a Commission who protects industry ... We've radically changed the public interest finding under the Act."[64]

According to *Television Digest*, as originally proposed by general counsel Stephen Sharp, the language of these recommendations did not include any mention of public interest. But commissioners Jones and Fogarty refused to vote on this original language. As Jones said, "under the statutes we have an obligation to do more than see if there's competition in the marketplace. Why else were we all appointed?"[65] Jones came up with new language and, along with Rivera and Washburn, voted for the change.

At this meeting, general counsel Sharp urged the commission to repeal provisions which he said were based on grounds that no longer existed, namely "scarcity of communications channels."[66] Fogarty disagreed and said he believed "the scarcity argument was still valid." But commissioner Dawson strongly endorsed repeal of the fairness doctrine and equal time provisions. She claimed "a dangerous precedent was set when we began with these ridiculous provisions. They're a danger to the First Amendment."[67] In the final voting on the commission's legislative recommendations, Fogarty and Washburn dissented to repealing fairness and equal time rules.

The battle had been joined, and where the parties stood identified. After the FCC meeting the Radio Television News Director Association (RTNDA) sent a letter to Fowler saying "this is possibly the most important step ever taken by the Commission to vindicate the public interest served by the First Amendment."[68] However, Friends of the Fairness Doctrine, an organization composed of a number of public interest groups, said "It's now official; the FCC has become the lobbying arm of the broadcasting industry... We're going to fight on this one -- real hard. Public resistance will be strong."[69]

Few believed Congress would agree to major portions of FCC legislative proposals. Representative Timothy Wirth (D-Colorado), Telecommunications Subcommittee chairman, said "speedy abolition is doubtful."[70] More importantly, though, the issues had been placed on the agenda. A crucial first step had been taken. And elimination of fairness doctrine did have influential Congressional advocates. For example, Republican Senators Packwood, Goldwater and Schmitt had all stated publicly they did not favor retaining fairness rules.[71]

In a September 23rd speech before the International Radio and Television Society in New York, Fowler gave the first public presentation of his redefinition of the public interest. The new FCC definition of public interest in broadcasting, Fowler said, moves away from the "trusteeship" mode of regulating industry toward a "marketplace approach."[72] "The FCC must deal with the reality of broadcasting ... that begins with the fact that broadcasting is a business."[73]

Disputing the traditional "trusteeship model" which he claimed was based on a scarcity argument, Fowler countered that the first amendment was a "more compelling reason" to abolish that approach. He claimed "economic freedom and freedom of speech go hand in hand." Fowler claimed substituting a "reliance on the marketplace eliminates areas in which government controls can be employed."[74] He urged, as he would throughout his term, that the broadcast industry support him in the repeal of the fairness doctrine and equal time provisions.

On October 22, 1981, the FCC issued a Notice of Proposed Rulemaking that sought to determine how teletext was to be regulated.[75]   One issue the commission said it was interested in looking at was whether teletext should be obligated by fairness doctrine considerations. Teletext used the vertical blanking interval of over-the-air broadcast signals. The vertical blanking interval is that portion of the television signal that appears as a black bar when the picture rolls. Examples of teletext service include news, weather reports, comparative shopping prices, entertainment schedules, closed captions for the hearing impaired, and business oriented information. This seemingly technical inquiry would have a significant impact on later FCC determinations of fairness doctrine considerations.

In a speech before the American Association of Advertising Agencies on October 26, 1981, Fowler again used his bully pulpit. He said "the historical justification used to explain the government's involvement with broadcasting no longer could sustain that involvement."[76] This involvement was scarcity, and he now sought to redefine it. He said scarcity, which historically had meant the shortage in the number of channels available for broadcast use was no longer valid. Rather, Fowler said, "scarcity is often the result of a shortage of advertising revenues, not of spectrum space."[77] He urged the members of American Association of Advertising Agencies actively support the commission's recommendation to remove the fairness doctrine and equal time provisions of the Communications Act.

Calling it "one of the most significant proposals for the deregulation of this nation's radio and TV broadcasting industry ever advanced in Congress," Representative Collins (R-Texas) introduced a series of bills (HR-4726, HR-4780, HR-4781) the last week of October which would have relaxed the fairness doctrine, eliminated equal time, ended limits on commercials, and made it tougher to challenge license renewals.[78]

Not all in Congress were ready for this type of action though. A House Telecommunications Subcommittee report was issued in the first week of November that urged Congress not to deregulate television.[79]   The report warned there was currently "disturbing indications that the present Commission believed a fully competitive market had already arrived and that it had no affirmative pro-competitive responsibility."[80]

Television Digest cited a mid-December letter to FCC chairman Mark Fowler from Senator Hollings (D-South Carolina), where he outlined a number of directives to the commission contained in a 1982 appropriations package. These directives included a "veiled warning" that the commission must not consider diverting any resources from policing of various political broadcasting laws.[81]

As Congress moved to adjourn for its Christmas recess, it passed, and President Reagan signed into law, a final budget resolution bill. As signed into law, Title XII of HR-3982 (PL 97-35) contained the following changes relevant to broadcasting:[82]

- Licenses. Increased television license terms to five years from three years. The terms would be extended for new licenses or renewals.
- Increased radio license terms to seven years from three years. The terms would be extended for new licenses or renewals.
- Directed the FCC to give "significant preference" to groups under-represented in broadcasting when it used a lottery system for granting new licenses.
- Changed the FCC's permanent authorization to a two-year period and authorized $76.9 million annually in fiscal 1982 and 1983.
- Required the FCC to appoint a managing director for overall commission management and to report its goals and priorities to Congress annually.

1982

1982 was particularly noteworthy for two reasons. First, it became obvious that when Fowler used the word "public" he really did not mean the general public. Rather he identified his "public" as those in the industries he was charged with regulating. And it was to this "public" he made his appeals. Second, 1982 saw Fowler increasingly alienating Congress. Not just Congressional Democrats, but also Republicans. He did this by trying to force his choice of commissioner, Stephen Sharp. Fowler showed a lack of understanding of the political nature of the process. This alienation, especially of key Congressional Republicans, would slow Fowler's deregulatory effort down.

By January 1982, Fowler was planning a reorganization plan for the full commission's consideration. This reorganization plan would combine several functions from both the Broadcast and the Cable bureaus. This new bureau would be responsible for all electronic media technologies, including some that were then part of the Common Carrier Bureau's domain. These included direct broadcast satellites (DBS), multi-point distribution services (MDS), as well as cable television which was under the Cable Bureau.[83] The person Fowler tapped to work out this reorganization plan was Laurence Harris. Harris took over as chief of the Broadcast Bureau on Monday, January 11. He shared many of Fowler's views on regulation. For example, he was quoted in a January 11, 1982, *Broadcasting* article saying, "I see my role as helping to shape a policy that gets the FCC out of the business of regulating program content."[84]

Mark Fowler, writing in a January 13, 1982, *Variety* piece, again took to the entertainment public his message calling for the abolition of the fairness doctrine. Telling it his FCC wanted to abolish the fairness doctrine, to remove "its camel's nose" from "under the program tent."[85] Of course, this was done in the name of the first amendment. In the same issue of *Variety*, Vincent T. Wasilewski, President of NAB, praised Fowler's September 23, 1981, IRTS speech.[86] Wasilewski said Fowler's call for the repeal of the fairness doctrine "offered the broadcasting industry the opportunity to establish its rights before Congress."[87]

Claiming the fairness doctrine had rendered the public interest subordinate to that of political tactics, Wasilewski said it had distorted the original Congressional intent. He called on broadcasting, as an industry, to ask Congress to extend it "the same high standards of the First Amendment now applied to the print media."[88]

The American Association of Advertising Agencies (AAAA), an organization who's membership perhaps had more at stake with respect to fairness doctrine applications, also issued a statement supporting the FCC's recommendation repealing the fairness doctrine.[89]

Addressing the National Religious Broadcasters on Tuesday, February 9, 1982, Fowler stated that "spectrum scarcity has been used as an excuse to regulate, not a reason!" His claim was that the technical theory of spectrum scarcity had been "employed as a camouflage ... to justify a dubious social theory."[90] An irony of this is that although maketplace theory is generally presented as an economic theory, the marketplace of ideas Fowler often alludes to is every bit as "dubious" a social theory.

And, in remarks before the Thomas Jefferson Award Dinner on Friday, February 19, 1982, Fowler ground his arguments justifying change by drawing historically on Thomas Jefferson and James Madison, and the Bill of Rights. He again argued against the trusteeship concept. Instead, he advocated his "marketplace approach." Rather than relying on the trustee model, he said, his "Commission will defer to a broadcaster's judgment about how best to compete for viewers and listeners, and how best to attract and sustain the public's interest."[91] He continued, "under this rationale, the public's interest defines the public interest in broadcasting."[92]

Fowler adhered to the philosophical *laissez faire* goal that served as an underpinning of the Reagan Administration. And, as he began to deal with major policy decisions and determinations in 1982, he did so with a relatively new cast of players. These included two new commission members, and new chiefs in both the Common Carrier Bureau and the Broadcast Bureau.[93]

Achieving his ends required a majority of a commission that supported him also. The commission was moving in that direction, but still did not conform perfectly. For example, Abbott Washburn, whose 7-year term on the FCC was to expire June 30, 1982, was the only Republican FCC member (along with Democrat Fogarty) who had voted against a Fowler proposal to seek Congressional repeal of the broadcast fairness doctrine.[94]

Ann P. Jones said that movement towards competitive markets must be done in a way that balances benefits to consumers against "the possibilities for anticompetitive abuse."[95] She was seen as keeping her own counsel and reaching her own decisions. She had been described as marching to the sound of "her own drummer."[96]

New Democratic commissioner Henry Rivera was viewed by some as a "token" Democrat, whose philosophic outlook actually was closer to that of President Reagan and FCC chairman Fowler than to many members of his own political party.[97]   At his Senate confirmation hearing Rivera, had said he agreed with the Reagan Administration's "commitment to the free market system" as an alternative to "costly, burdensome and unnecessary regulation." He described himself as "pro-business" and "pro-deregulation."[98]

Quello, also a Democrat, was known to be an even more ardent supporter of these policies. He had long been vigorous in advocating for broadcasters the same first amendment rights enjoyed by the print press.[99]

Many believed Mary Ann (Mimi) Weyforth Dawson, a Republican, was destined some day to become chairperson of the FCC.[100] Her confirmation hearing itself provided an indication that Dawson had considerable support in official Washington. She had the backing of Senator Robert Packwood, chairman of the Commerce Committee. He described a major strength of hers as having an "appreciation of the legislative process."

Only one commissioner rejected outright the marketplace theory now pursued by the commission. Commissioner Joseph Fogarty, the last liberal Democrat serving on the commission, said, "We still license the spectrum."[101]   Citizen groups were also becoming increasingly worried. For example, the National Citizens Committee for Broadcasting's Sam Simon saw Fowler conducting an "anti-First Amendment, anticonsumer program."[102]

Whatever their reactions, though, virtually everyone was impressed with the swift and decisive manner with which Fowler moved to place his stamp on the commission. And he had put in key staff positions people of his choice who all agreed with his approach to regulation.[103] Fowler, as chairman, was to prove a quite effective leader. He was a persuasive lobbyist who controlled the commission agenda.

On Friday, February 19, general counsel Stephen Sharp and Broadcast Bureau chief Harris made a joint proposal. They proposed that rulings on complaints involving the fairness doctrine and equal time be shifted from the Complaints and Compliance Division of FCC's Broadcast Bureau to the General Counsel's Office. This was a highly controversial plan. The general counsel is political appointee, and many inside and outside the commission felt that rulings under Section 315 should not be made by an office headed by an individual who owed his job to politics.[104]   NCCB Executive Director Samuel Simon, characterized this proposal as an attempt by Fowler, "to gut enforcement and administration of equal time and fairness since he is on record as opposing both."[105]

Enforcement of the fairness doctrine and equal time had been the responsibility of Complaints and Compliance since the division was formed in 1960. Milton Gross headed the Fairness/Political Broadcasting Branch. Under the Sharp/Harris proposal the entire unit would move to General Counsel's Office. But commissioner Joseph Fogarty disagreed. He said the Fairness/Political Broadcasting Branch should remain in the Broadcast Bureau, and he criticized the staff proposal in a memo he circulated to his fellow commissioners.[106]

According to *Broadcasting*, Fogarty's memo said, "no other area of commission responsibility is of higher political sensitivity and visibility, and in my judgment the credibility of commission decisions depends in large measure on maintaining the present organizational structure and process."[107]   He contended that the transfer would eliminate the commission's current "dual review" of fairness and political broadcasting issues.[108]   "The fundamental consideration, however, is the need to maintain the credibility and integrity of the decision-making process of Section 315 and fairness doctrine matters which the existing organizational structure safeguards and insures," Fogarty said.[109]

Claiming he was attempting to "remove the noose of government regulation from broadcasters,"[110] Representative Broyhill (R-North Carolina) introduced a two-bill package (HR-5595) the last week of February. Broyhill's proposal called for major deregulation ranging from repeal of the fairness doctrine to elimination of comparative license renewal procedure.

Specifically, Broyhill's proposed legislation included:

(1)   Repeal of fairness doctrine and equal time law.

(2)   Stripping FCC of authority to revoke licenses for broadcasting obscene material.

(3)   Pro-competitive amendment to Communications Act urging FCC to strive for "creation of competitive environment."

(4)   Replacing comparative license renewal with petition-to-deny process.

(5)   Open meetings law would not apply to certain meetings between FCC or other government agencies and foreign entities.

(6)   Ascertainment, advertising limits and other programming guidelines would be eliminated for both radio and TV.

(7)   FCC fines for violations of Communications Act would be increased from current maximum of $20,000 to $100,000.[111]

Fowler spoke at the NATPE convention in Las Vegas during the third week of March.   As *Television Digest* reported it, "Fowler echoed what had become the theme of his tenure."   He promised to "make good" on first amendment rights for broadcasters.[112]

Fowler, writing in an April 1982, issue of *Communications News*, reviewed his short term as chairman.[113]   He said he had attempted to infuse the agency with a clear purpose.   He again stressed the need to end regulating broadcasting under the "so-called trusteeship model," and instead move to a marketplace approach.   Fowler claimed that "under the trusteeship notion, the Commission assumed that it should fashion the rules by which broadcasters would serve their communities."[114]

He said under his marketplace approach to broadcast regulation, "the Commission should defer to a broadcaster's judgment about how best to compete for viewers and listeners."   He again stressed that under his marketplace approach, "the public's interest defines the public interest in broadcasting."[115]

This idea was also stressed in his address to the NAB convention on April 7, 1982, in Dallas, Texas.[116]   Drawing on the first amendment, he called the fairness doctrine and equal time laws a form of government censorship.   He urged broadcasters to support Representative James Broyhill's recently introduced legislation.

Six FCC commissioners also appeared on a panel at the NAB convention.   There, Fowler's view were also supported.   Commissioner Quello again called for first amendment rights for broadcasters.   He said the FCC should be "in spectrum management and engineering enforcement and get rid of everything else."[117]   Commissioner Washburn, however, said he did not think broadcasters were "fettered."[118]   But commissioner Jones disagreed.   She said she saw the fairness doctrine as "a serious infringement of a very important constitutional right."[119]   Perhaps the biggest surprise came when commissioner Rivera said that since fairness doctrine was produced by FCC, not Congress, "I don't see why we couldn't put out a notice of inquiry and rulemaking" to address it, rather than wait for legislation.[120]   Not surprisingly, broadcasters were quick to respond to this.

Fowler, in an April 12 *U.S. News & World Report* interview, characterized the FCC as "the last of the New Deal dinosaurs" that had outlived its usefulness. Fowler said the agency should be nothing more than a technical traffic cop when it comes to broadcasting, and he said he viewed the fairness doctrine as a disincentive to free speech.[121]

The support Fowler was finding with broadcasters was not wholly mirrored in Congress. His first major confrontation with Congress took the form of a battle between the Administration and Senate over who should be nominated to replace FCC commissioner Washburn. This battle was to cost Fowler even Republican Congressional support. Fowler lobbied hard for his general counsel Stephen Sharp to get the vacant commission seat, and Reagan chose to support Fowler.[122]

But Senators Ted Stevens (R-Alaska), Bob Packwood (R-Oregon) and Barry Goldwater (R-Arizona) had told Reagan to abandon his choice of FCC nominee and substitute theirs. They recommended Marvin Weatherly, an Alaska Public Utilities commissioner. The roots of the conflict went back to Mimi Weyforth Dawson's nomination. Then Stevens and Packwood had made a deal to trade FCC nominees. Stevens supported Packwood's aide, Mimi Weyforth Dawson, for the first appointment to the FCC under the Republican administration. In exchange Packwood promised to support Stevens' nominee, Marvin Weatherly to the second FCC vacancy.[123] But Reagan ignored their choice, and instead backed Fowler's recommendation of Stephen Sharp, the FCC's general counsel.

Packwood said publicly that the Commerce Committee, which he headed, would hold no confirmation hearing for any FCC nominee except Stevens.[124] Neither Reagan nor Packwood would back down. And, at a meeting with Senator Stevens (R-Alaska) in the White House on Monday, April 19th, President Reagan flat-out said that he intended to appoint his choice, FCC general counsel Stephen Sharp, as commissioner.[125]

On Wednesday, May 15, 1982, Reagan announced his intention to nominate Stephen A. Sharp to be a member of the FCC for a term of 7 years from July 1, 1982.[126] He would succeed Abbott Washburn. Sharp had previously been a staff attorney in the Office of the General Counsel at the FCC in 1974-76, and had been legal assistant to FCC commissioner Margita E. White in 1976-78. From 1978 to 1981 he was an attorney at law with the firm of Schnader, Harrison, Segal and Lewis, Washington, D.C.

Sharp, like Fowler, was regarded as a conservative who believed strongly in deregulation. Also like Fowler, Sharp believed the marketplace was the best determinant of the public interest.[127] Sharp's nomination was viewed as a demonstration of the influence Fowler wielded at the White House. Fowler strongly backed Sharp for the post. Sharp also had been strongly endorsed by Jerry Falwell's Moral Majority.[128]

Before Reagan officially announced his nomination of Sharp, the Senate Commerce Committee began considering reducing the number of FCC commissioners from seven to five. This was to be a classic political confrontation. Packwood was unable to get Reagan to budge, and so he would resolve the dispute by appointing no one.[129]

Key Republican lawmakers became outraged with the role Fowler had in pushing for Sharp's nomination. *Telephony* reported Fowler had even asked some lobbyists who dealt with the commission to approach their contacts in Congress and the White House to seek support for Sharp.[130]

Fowler released a 16-page memorandum listing his first year accomplishments in the middle of May. The memorandum, prepared by Edward J. Minkel, managing director, was organized in terms of the five basic objectives adopted when Fowler assumed the chairmanship.[131]

In all, the memorandum listed 74 accomplishment. 24 were included under the first objective, "to create, to the maximum extent possible, an unregulated, competitive marketplace environment for the development of telecommunications." 17 accomplishments were listed under the second objective, "to eliminate unnecessary regulation and policies." The list included specific proposals in the "Track I" (minor) and "Track II" (major) legislative proposals the commission submitted to Congress. Under the third objective, "to provide service to the public in the most efficient, expedition manner possible," Minkel listed 22 accomplishments. Included were steps creating the management-by-objective program described in the memorandum. As for efforts to "promote the coordination and planning of international communications which assures the vital interests of the American public in commerce, defense and foreign policy," Fowler's fourth objective, the report listed 10 accomplishments.[132]

Objective five, "to eliminate government action that infringes the freedom of the speech and the press," contained only three accomplishments. These were the proposals, contained in "Track II" legislative proposals (and listed early under Objective 2 accomplishments), that called for the removal of provisions that applied to political candidates, and for repeal of the equal-time and fairness doctrine provisions of Section 315 of the Communications Act.[133] The memorandum said the commission's "intrusion into the First Amendment" was required by statute and that, as a result, the agency's effort to avoid interfering with free speech was limited to the legislative proposals.[134]

Specifically, Fowler described commission action on Objective Five as:[135]

-- Proposed legislation reducing Government involvement in content regulation, by removing reasonable access, equal time, and Fairness Doctrine provisions.

-- Instituted an Inquiry into a less restrictive interpretation of the equal time rules.

-- Instructed the General Counsel to examine Commission regulations imposing restrictions on freedom of speech and recommend strategies for ending them.

Fowler continued his public crusade in a speech before the First Amendment Congress in Leesburg, Virginia, on May 20, 1982, questioning whether a right of public access to commercial television was appropriate under the trusteeship model. Constructing his own interpretation of a 1973 Supreme Court case, *CBS, Inc. V. Democratic National Committee*,[136] Fowler claimed the Supreme Court ruled that there was no right of access. He claimed the *CBS* case emphasized function over form, and that what "the first amendment is concerned with is creative activity, editorial enterprise."[137] Fowler makes no mention of a right of the public to access to ideas.

By a unanimous voice vote Wednesday, June 2, 1982, the House Commerce Committee approved, and sent to the floor, the FCC "Track I" bill (HR-5008).[138] This bill, which had bipartisan support, provided for most of the commission requested changes in its operations. Representative Wirth (D-Colorado), Telecommunications Subcommittee chairman, in urging its passage, said the bill would eliminate paperwork, improve FCC efficiency and save money in some areas.[139] Key provisions of HR-5008 were essentially the same as those in a Senate-passed bill, S-929. Final passage of the House version by both chambers of Congress was expected.[140] However, the controversial "Track II" amendments, which included repeal of the fairness doctrine and other political broadcasting laws, received no action by the Telecommunications Subcommittee.[141]

Failing to get legislative action on his "Track II" proposals, FCC chairman Mark Fowler in the last week of June carried his fight for "full" first amendment rights for broadcasters to the op-ed page of the *Washington Post*. *Broadcasting* claimed Fowler was aiming his remarks at fellow conservative Republicans who, he said, were surprised by his insistence on first amendment rights for broadcasters. "Some notable conservatives believe that more, not less, restraint should be imposed on broadcast news organizations, particularly network television, which they view as biased against conservatives.[142] Fowler continued, "I feel that it is correct constitutionally and as a conservative to support less, not more restraint, on the press. To my mind, true conservatism means less involvement by the government in the lives and affairs of people. Content regulation of broadcasting is out of place in this scheme."[143]

In a short-lived recommendation, that actually made sense, FCC chairman Fowler suggested charging commercial broadcasters for the "exclusivity" provided by government license. In return, public broadcasters would assume responsibility of satisfying public programming needs. This suggestion came in a *Texas Law Review* article authored by Fowler and his legal assistant and part-time speech writer, Daniel Brenner.[144] They contended that broadcasters should be considered as marketplace participants rather than "fiduciaries" of public airwave, because only this approach could insure full first amendment rights. The article reserved for public broadcasting most of the public interest programming requirements then considered license requirements for commercial broadcasters. They said: "Having decided to distort the market at the outset by reserving a number of spectrum exclusivities for [public] broadcasting, it follows that the FCC can make some provision for programs that might not find their way on the air through market mechanism... Commercial broadcasters would be absolutely free to pursue commercial objectives without lingering trusteeship obligations. At the same time, noncommercial broadcasters would have a clear mandate to provide service alternative to, not duplicative of, the types of programming available over commercial channels."[145]

These suggestions may have seemed logical. But given the reality of Reagan's disdain for government funding of public broadcasting, and commercial broadcasters opposition to funding what it they viewed as their competition, it was not surprising these suggestions went nowhere.

Legislation was attached to the Commerce Committee's budget reconciliation package for fiscal 1983 (S-2774), by Senator Harrison Schmitt (R-New Mexico) in the middle of June. Specifically, Schmitt proposed reducing the number of FCC commissioners from seven to five on June 30, 1982. *Broadcasting* quoted Schmitt as saying the legislation was "needed to cut costs."[146] But no one was fooled by the politics involved.

By now, using the budget reconciliation process rather than direct legislation was becoming standard fare. For example, the Senate Commerce Committee had the year before used that reconciliation bill as the vehicle for legislation lengthening broadcast license terms and for new authorizing legislation for public broadcasting.[147]

Senator Packwood (R-Oregon) also announced in July his plans to hold field hearings in the fall in New York. He sought to gain views of the industry and public on a Constitutional amendment to extend first amendment rights to the electronic media.[148] He also announced that another hearing would be held at an unspecified later date in Los Angeles.

Another bureau reorganization plan emerged at the last commission meeting in July. This plan would rename the Broadcast Bureau the Electronic Media Bureau. Under this reorganization plan the Bureau would take over regulation of MDS and fixed services from Common Carrier Bureau. Both of these would go into a new division handling video services. The Cable Bureau would be merged into a new division of the Broadcast Bureau. Complaints and Compliance Division would remain with the new Electronic Media Bureau, instead of being shifted to the General Counsel Office as had been suggested by Harris and Sharp in February.[149]

Following only a few minutes of debate, the Senate voted Thursday, August 5, to reduce the size of the FCC from seven members to five. This came attached to the omnibus budget reconciliation bill (S-2774), and its passage came despite Reagan administration objections.

Broadcasting reported that repeatedly Presidential staffers had tried to convince the proposal's primary proponents, Commerce Committee chairman Bob Packwood (R-Oregon), Communications Subcommittee Chairman Barry Goldwater (R-Arizona) and Senators Ted Stevens (R-Alaska) and Harrison Schmitt (R-New Mexico), to reverse their stand. Also, according to *Broadcasting*, Fowler had "further irritated the committee" by working to defeat the FCC reduction proposal.[150] *Television Digest* reported that although the White House had opposed reducing the number of commissioners, few believed Reagan would veto the spending bill because of the small section dealing with the FCC.[151]

Only days after Congress voted to reduce the size of the commission, on Thursday, August 19, Congress gave the FCC a major victory. Congress passed the commission's "Track I" legislative proposals.[152] According to *Television Digest*, this was the first time a major piece of FCC-pushed and originated legislation had cleared Congress since 1960.[153]

Fowler, citing his *Texas Law Review* article in an address before the National Radio Broadcasters Association on September 13, 1982, in Reno, Nevada,[154] attempted to clarify what he meant by "spectrum fees and their relationship to a marketplace approach." He said these fees could be earmarked specifically for:

> public radio and television, whose programming mission could supplement, not duplicate, the offerings of commercial broadcasters. Whether it's educational children's programming or long-form radio news programs, there's a job for public broadcasting to do in a deregulated environment.[155]

Broadcasters were less than eager to jump on this bandwagon. Funding their competition was more than they were willing to do.

The next day, Tuesday, September 14, 1982, as expected, the FCC, meeting in closed session agreed to expand the Broadcast Bureau's authority and give it a new name.[156] The bureau was to be known as the Mass Media Bureau, and it combined the former Broadcast and Cable Television Bureaus into one.

Under the reorganization, the Broadcast Bureau's six divisions and the Cable Television Bureau's five divisions were collapsed into four division in the new bureau. William Johnson, chief of the Cable

Television Bureau, became deputy chief of the Mass Media Bureau, and reported to Larry Harris, Mass Media Bureau chief. Henry (Jeff) Baumann, former deputy chief of the Broadcast Bureau, remained a deputy chief under the reorganization.[157]

Chief of the new audio services division was Larry Eads. The chief of the new video services division was Roy Stewart, chief of the former renewal and transfer division. The video services division consisted of four branches - cable, distribution services, low-power television and television.

The political/fairness branch combined the Broadcast and Cable Bureau functions in this area into one. The Enforcement Division would have several branches: Complaints, Equal Employment Opportunity, Fairness/Political Broadcasting, Hearing and Investigative.[158]

An unusually long nomination hearing was finally held for Stephen Sharp, Wednesday, September 22, 1982.[159] In a prepared statement, Sharp elaborated on his definition of public interest. He said, "I have concluded that generally the public interest is served best where Government is least involved in interfering with either the economic marketplace or the marketplace of ideas."[160] When asked if he supported repeal of the fairness doctrine and section 315 of the Communication Act, Sharp simply replied, "Yes."[161]

There were many at Sharp's hearing speaking against his confirmation. For example, in a prepared statement John Hemenway, Assistant to the Chairman, Accuracy in Media, Inc., quoted a May 24, 1982, *Broadcasting* article which gave insight into Sharp's views on enforcing the fairness doctrine:

> And if he is uncomfortable with some of the rules and laws on the books, he says that has not stopped him and will not from seeing that they are enforced. That is his duty. But it won't always be with enthusiasm. As for the Fairness Doctrine, for instance, which he feels has lost any constitutional basis it ever had, he contends the scarcity argument has been overtaken by events, specifically, the vast increase in the number and kinds of media. "You hold your nose and you enforce it.[162]

Hemenway implored the committee, "don't send a man out to administer a program you really want enforced if he doesn't agree with the program."[163] Sharp's nomination was opposed by most public interest groups. But he received Congressional approval nonetheless.

In an September 27th interview with *Broadcasting* editors, chairman Fowler sought to further clarify his spectrum-use charge to benefit public broadcasting.[164] He called on broadcasters to agree to pay a "modest" fee in exchange for statutory deregulation.[165]

Fowler had initiated this meeting. He wanted to respond to a *Broadcasting* editorial which had commented negatively on his NRBA speech. This was the speech where he had raised the subject of a spectrum-use fee. But now Fowler had already begun distancing himself from his own proposal. Fowler said he was fixed on the concept of using fees more or less as only a bargaining chip. He said he thought this might help get broadcast deregulation codified. And he exhorted broadcasters to push for statutory deregulation now, since the current FCC "isn't going to be around forever."[166]

John Summers, executive vice president and general manager of the NAB, typified the broadcast industry ability to talk out of both sides of its mouth. He said that while NAB was "committed" to doing everything it could to help public broadcasting, it didn't "believe in taxing commercial broadcasters to support public broadcasting."[167]

September 28 and 30, 1982, Senator Packwood held his public hearings to garner support for his Free Expression Constitutional Amendment.[168] The list of invited witnesses were overwhelmingly in support of the proposal. Witnesses for these hearings, and the third public hearing held November 19, 1982, included: Dr. Solomon Buchsbaum, executive vice president, Bell Telephone Laboratories; Dr. John Harrington, senior vice president, research and development, and director, Comsat Laboratories; Dr. Charles Jackson, Shooshan & Jackson; Harry E. Smith, vice president, technology, CBS, Inc.; Professor Thomas Krattenmaker, professor of law, Georgetown University Law Center; Professor Ithiel de Sola Pool, Massachusetts Institute of Technology; Professor William Van Alstyne, Duke University Law School; Karl Eller; Bill Monroe, moderator and executive producer, Meet the Press, NBC News; and Dan Rather, CBS News.

Mark Fowler had originally hoped broadcasters would see his reasoning for spectrum fees and actively support his proposal. The support never materialized. His speech before the Radio Television News Directors Association, October 1, 1982, in Las Vegas, Nevada,[169] already began showing his movement away from the idea.

He began by deconstructing the 1969 *Red Lion* decision. He claimed it:

> Relied on the supposed scarcity of broadcasting frequencies to justify regulation. . . . Any of us could walk out of this room and apply for these stations, assuming there was capital to support a new venture. Typically there is insufficient advertising or other revenues to support an additional outlet in these markets. That reason, not some shortage of ether, is the real reason why there are fewer stations in smaller markets than otherwise might be.[170]

By now Fowler was already willing to back away from the spectrum fee. He said he advanced it to "break the ice" in the deregulation discussions.[171] Hoping to salvage some support he said "this user fee would be imposed not alone on broadcasters, but on all users of the spectrum."[172]

And in a speech to the North Carolina Association of Broadcasters in Raleigh on October 25, the spectrum proposal became even less pronounced.[173] Fowler again fell back on the phrase "the public's interest defines the public interest."[174] He promised to "do everything in my power at the FCC, consistent with legislation on the books," to continue to move to deregulate both TV and radio.[175] He reiterated the need for new statutes, "passed by Congress, to get the job done... and to prevent a different Commission from turning the clock backwards."[176] And even though he asked the North Carolina broadcasters to urge the NAB to withdraw its opposition and actively support a user fee, no action would be forthcoming. While Fowler had presented his rationale for considering the support of fees in several different forums, support for the concept in Congress and by broadcasters never materialized.

In a November 15, 1982, question and answer interview with *Barron's*,[177] Mark Fowler again took the opportunity to publicly air his views. Here he focussed on why he believed a print model for broadcast was appropriate; why he opposed the fairness doctrine; and why spectrum fees were desirable.

As to the print model for broadcasters, he said "broadcasters should be as free as the newspapers or magazines; they shouldn't have any of these rules."[178] Saying the FCC was limited in terms of eliminating content control, because "the most onerous restrictions are derived from statutes passed by Congress," he said why he opposed the fairness doctrine and equal time laws:

Why do we need a fairness doctrine? If we look at the newspapers, we find that, generally speaking, they present all sides of controversial issues in their straight news coverage, because marketplace forces impel them to do so.[179]

When asked if broadcast and print aren't fundamentally different, he draws on his redefinition of scarcity. He said:

The old argument about the scarcity of the airwaves no longer apply, but even 10 years ago I would have said, "Get rid of the fairness doctrine." When the founding fathers came up with the First Amendment, there were eight weekly newspapers in the entire country, and yet they said, "These eight shall be free." They didn't do a scarcity analysis. There are about 1,100 commercial television stations now. There's cable TV. We have authorized direct broadcast satellites. We have video discs, video cassettes, microwave television in some of the major cities now. Low-power television is coming along. Pay cable is a growing offshoot of cable. Over-the-air pay is taking hold in many markets, and doing very well--growing exponentially.

So what scarcity are we talking about when we look and compare all this to about 1,600 daily newspapers, total, in the country?[180]

Finally, when asked to explain why "the free-enterprise chairman of the FCC supports a government subsidy for public broadcasting," he said:

Economists recognize that there are certain things they call merit goods, that a marketplace may not provide but that the society may want or need. Some examples are libraries, public museums, public schools, public parks. And, I happen to believe, public broadcasting is one of those merit goods. It seems to me that there is a place for it in our society and that it's not inconsistent with our reliance on the marketplace to recognize those exceptions. And I think this may be something that the people would say is worthwhile.[181]

Unfortunately, he never followed through on this.

As 1982 closed, the composition of the FCC looked like this:[182]

Member	Party	Term Expires	Nominated	Confirmed by Senate
Mark S. Fowler	R	6/30/86	4/27/81	5/14/81
Joseph R. Fogarty	D	6/30/83	6/21/76	9/8/76
James H. Quello	D	6/30/84	7/8/81	7/31/81
Anne P. Jones	R	6/30/85	1/15/79	3/21/79
Henry M. Rivera	D	6/30/87	7/8/81	7/31/81
Mary Ann Weyforth-Dawson	R	6/30/88	5/12/81	6/4/81
Stephen A. Sharp	R	6/30/83	5/24/82	10/1/82

1983

The most significant communications event with long-term consequences for the fairness doctrine occurring in 1983 was a seemingly technical commission determination.   The commission concluded that teletext should be exempted from fairness doctrine obligations.   The determination itself was not as significant as the language of the commission report.   Other significant events in 1984 were the appointment of Bruce Fein as general counsel; the commission moving on television deregulation; and the appointment of Dennis Patrick as commissioner.

As *Broadcasting* said of Bruce Fein, FCC general counsel designate, on January 10, 1983, "if the man the FCC installed as its general counsel can offer further evidence of where the commission is going, broadcasters should be reassured."[183] The statement was truly prophetic. Bruce E. Fein, 35, officially moved in as general counsel on Monday, January 3, 1983. He made it clear that he, like chairman Mark Fowler, had an aversion to government regulation and an affectation for the marketplace.[184]

Fein, unlike his predecessors who saw their role of general counsel as one of principally offering legal advice, believed the general counsel should directly affect commission policy. This change had begun with Stephen Sharp, but it was to find new meaning with Fein. He especially questioned laws and regulations used to regulate content; believing the fairness doctrine and the equal opportunities rules, "ought to carry a heavy presumption of suspicion under the First Amendment."[185]

Fein said in an *Broadcasting* interview, "I'm not someone who genuflects to past precedent." He continued, "I'm not reluctant to ask the courts or administrative agencies to overrule their past decisions, if the factual premises obtained [in a particular case] no longer obtain or the logic [behind those cases] has not passed the test of time."[186]

Fein's previous experience with the fairness doctrine had come working on a Justice Department brief for a 1979 case in which the Court of Appeals, Washington, affirmed the commission's dismissal of a fairness doctrine complaint by the American Security Council Education Foundation against CBS News coverage of national security matters.[187]

Fein's first public speech as general counsel came January 20, 1983. He addressed the Federal Communications Bar Association in Washington.[188] He confirmed he was a full-fledged advocate of chairman Fowler's "unregulation" views. Fein said Fowler had "enlisted ... competition to bestow incalculably economic and political benefits on the nation and to make customers and listeners the stewards of the ideas, products and services generated by the telecommunications industry."[189]

Fein also clarified his views on broadcast deregulation: "I believe that the *Red Lion* [decision] should be overruled, that Congress should repeal the fairness doctrine as expressly embodied in Section 315... and that the Commission should discard its personal attack and political editorializing rules."[190] He claimed that the troublesome questions "raised by the fairness doctrine have been received with general taciturnity by the broadcast industry is indicative of the intimidating effects of government regulation."[191]

Senator William Proxmire (D-Wisconsin) announced the second week of January that he would again introduce a bill to abolish the fairness doctrine and equal time law. Proxmire had introduced similar measures in 1975, 1977, 1979 and 1981. The measure would be called the First Amendment Clarification Act of 1983.[192]

Proxmire had long held that the fairness doctrine and equal time law violated the first amendment. As quoted in *Broadcasting* on January 17, 1983, he said "The doctrine ... does not stimulate the free expression of diverse ideas. Rather, it promotes the 'sameness' of ideas. Stations avoid the airing of controversial issues because they fear a challenge to their license renewal or expensive litigation resulting from a fairness complaint."[193] He also dismissed the idea that government regulation was necessary because of spectrum scarcity.

Fowler, in January 1983, also returned his responses to follow-up questions requested by Representative Dingell (D-Michigan). Dingell had submitted 33 questions to Fowler as a follow-up to a Telecommunications Subcommittee's December 1, 1982, FCC oversight hearing.[194] Fowler said the FCC was pursuing deregulation because it was "mandated" by Congress to look into television deregulation.[195]

Also contained in these responses were figures on the number of fairness doctrine and equal time complaints filed in 1982, and actions taken on them by the commission. According to Fowler, there were a total of 1,278 fairness doctrine and equal time complaints filed in 1982. Of these 1,278 complaints 31 were referred to licensees, and 18 rulings were made adverse to licensees.[196]

At a March 9, 1983, FCC authorization hearing before the Senate Commerce Committee, Senator Hollings expressed his reservations about the current FCC's enforcement of political broadcasting laws. As he said:[197]

> I am greatly concerned about the Commission's, and, in particular, the Chairman's commitment to effectively administering and enforcing the political broadcasting laws.

Hollings said this concern was based on the fact that "We all know that the Commission has recommended the repeal of these laws."[198] He continued, that:

> While Commissioners may claim they will faithfully execute the laws, I cannot but help to be extremely wary of those advocating repeal also overseeing the effectiveness of the laws. To add credence to my cause for concern the Commission has made the administration and enforcement to these laws a "C" priority. There are no lower priorities.

Fowler never directly addressed Senator Hollings' concern. Rather he spoke generally of the commissions accomplishments during his term, and their plans for further deregulation.[199]

The ANPA telecommunications committee recommended to the board of directors of the American Newspaper Publishers Association that it adopt a policy advocating repeal of equal time and the fairness doctrine. The committee made its decision at a March 9-11 meeting in Washington, D.C.[200]

After over four years as a commissioner, Anne P. Jones, a Republican appointed by former President Jimmy Carter, announced her intention to resign by May 31.[201] Her departure raised the obvious question of who would be the new variable in the commission's power equation? This also left James Quello as the only one of five remaining commissioners not appointed by Reagan.

Mark Fowler, speaking at the closing luncheon of the NAB convention in Las Vegas the second week in April, described a bright world of opportunity awaiting broadcasters. "It is a world filled with potential profit centers and made possible by technology and the commission's policy of permitting broadcasters to participate in the new businesses being created," he said.[202] His discussion focussed on what he saw as six targets of business opportunities. He listed these six areas as: (1) subcarrier authorization; (2) broadcast auxiliary; (3) teletext; (4) MDS; (5) cellular radio; and (6) cable leasing.[203]

Fortuitously, he said of teletext, "I think history will record 1983 as the year we scratched the surface in the possible applications of teletext [authorized by the commission three weeks ago] and other video services to be transmitted by way of the vertical blanking interval."[204]

At a news conference following his speech, Fowler announced the FCC would take up an NAB petition to abolish personal attack rule during its April 24 meeting. And, at a follow-up convention session, Mass Media Bureau Chief Laurence Harris predicted the current commission would vote to abolish the rule.

The main focus of the convention was on two issues: (1) Congressional codification of deregulatory steps already taken by the FCC: and (2) broadcasters' adamant opposition to inclusion of spectrum fees in such legislation.[205]

Senator Packwood also sought to rally support for his own legislative initiative (S-55) at the NAB convention. The bill had passed the Senate, and Packwood said it accomplished what broadcasters wanted. But, he said, the bill was languishing the House because of insistence of Telecommunications Subcommittee Chairman Wirth that legislation include a spectrum fee. This led Packwood to criticize the NAB, saying it "couldn't lobby itself out of a paper bag in the House".[206]   According to Packwood, the NAB had failed "to deliver" on broadcast deregulation in Congress. He concluded by saying, "I sometimes wonder if broadcasters really want out from under the [program] content rules."[207]

Growing tension between the FCC and Congress were apparent at an April 19, House Telecommunications Subcommittee oversight hearing.[208]   At times, the session degenerated into a shouting match between Fowler and panel member Representative Leland (D-Texas) over affirmative action hiring, with Fowler denying he was a racist.[209] Fowler also was questioned by Representative Dingell (D-Michigan) over his interpretation of the meaning of the public interest standard.[210]

Questions of television and radio deregulation also came up. As Representative Timothy Wirth was warning Fowler against taking premature action, Fowler was arguing the issue of television and radio deregulation could be divorced from action on spectrum fees. Wirth wanted spectrum fee legislation in order to get deregulation approved by Congress. Fowler was obviously backing off from earlier strong statements in support of the fee to help fund public broadcasting. He now said fees should only be among a range of ideas to be considered.[211]

At a Society of Professional Journalists regional conference in Portland, Oregon, the third week in April, commissioner Dawson warned journalists of threats to the first amendment brought on by new electronic media such as teletext. She said, "the First Amendment is today being eroded, and that erosion is a direct result of the technological advances which have blurred the distinctions between press and electronic media."[212]

Dawson cautioned print journalists that they could no longer afford to be "indifferent" to first amendment restrictions on broadcasters. She continued, that while the FCC was powerless to repeal equal time and fairness doctrine restrictions in Communications Act, the agency "can start to remove some of the regulatory baggage that surround the fairness doctrine and political broadcasting consistent... with the law."[213]

FCC commissioner Stephen Sharp announced on April 28, that he would not seek to serve beyond June 30. This was when his current term was due to expire.[214]   Fowler had produced a major rift between the Reagan Administration and powerful Congressional Republicans by his insistence on advancing Sharp's nomination, as well as further straining FCC and Congressional relations. But according to a *Television Digest* report, since becoming commissioner, Sharp and Fowler had a falling out. In retrospect it would certainly seem the loss of support caused in the process was not worth the final result.

As indicated in Fowler's April NAB address, and certainly evidenced by commission action, Fowler seemed quite concerned with removing restrictions on existing firms that would encourage competition. But the commission was less willing to expand the ability of new firms to offer existing services where true competition could come about most rapidly. Rather, the Fowler commission had focused its attention on creating new services that were either secondary to existing services; or structures so they could only supplement and not compete with existing services; or were able to compete only far in the future.

The commission increasingly relied on the argument that technological distinctions were blurring legal precedents. Its claim was the three bodies of law had which grown up around the three different traditional categories of communications technology were loosing their validity. For the print media, a British-inherited tradition of almost no regulation evolved. For telephone, telegraph, and postal services, the status of "common carrier," had evolved. The common carrier model permits monopoly but is supposed to guarantee nondiscriminatory access. For the third model, that of broadcasting, a regulatory scheme that combined elements of private freedoms and public obligations developed. Fowler's FCC contended the new technologies had put strains on all three of these models, especially on the last. Its mechanism for resolving these technological distinctions was the marketplace. But there is a distinction necessary between the marketplace as a goal or guiding principal, and the marketplace as a reality.

The *New Republic* may have best summarized this approach when it said "Letting the marketplace do the FCC's work is like having the referee go home so that the strongest contender can dictate the rules of the fight."[215] As it pointed out, in 1983 more than a third of all American households had annual incomes of less that $15,000, and "the marketplace, particularly the advertiser-supported media, cares little for them." This led the *New Republic* to conclude that the first amendment flag was being waved less for constitutional than for financial reasons.[216]

The FCC issued a rulemaking at its meeting in the second week of May to change or eliminate the personal attack and political editorial rules for broadcasters.[217] Its decision came after it had made an initial determination that those rules were not accomplishing their intended goals.[218] This action had come in direct response to the April petition from the NAB.

In his presentation to the commissioners, FCC general counsel Bruce Fein said the rules were not working. He said the personal attack rule was being used by "victims" to get free air time instead of them filing defamation of character lawsuits. This, Fein claimed, unjustly limited the discretion of licensees.[219] Of the political editorial rule, Fein said it "appears to be inhibiting" political endorsements by television stations. Fein said the FCC's "tentative view" was "we want to encourage editorial" endorsements. His rationale was that it would probably be better for viewers to know which candidates a stations supports and evaluate news coverage on that basis.[220]

The commission, in taking up the NAB petition, stated that courts have "recognized that the FCC actions which interfere with licensee's programming discretion by giving specific individuals a right to use broadcaster's facilities, are contrary to the policies of the Communications Act."[221] These conclusions were not shared by all commissioners though. Commissioners Rivera and Fogarty said they would only concur with the commission decision. Fogarty said the rulemaking "minimizes the fact that *Red Lion* is still the law. Scarcity is still the law." Chairman Fowler and commissioners Quello and Dawson though strongly supported the move.[222]

Though made effective from March 31, 1983, the FCC released Monday, June 13, 1983, its Report and Order on teletext services.[223] This was to be one of the most significant documents in its "war" against the fairness doctrine. Because buried in its seemingly technical authorization was an undocumented conclusion that served as the basis for the doctrine's later dismissal.

By way of summary, the Report and Order authorized television stations to operate teletext services on the vertical blanking interval of the television video signal. This authorization came about as a result of consideration in a Notice of Proposed Rule Making in 1981 (BC Docket 81-741, 48 Fed. Reg. 60851, adopted October 22, 1981, published December 14, 1981). As a result of this Notice of Proposed Rule Making, the commission concluded that the public interest would be served by allowing television broadcasters to engage in teletext services.[224]

What follows is a summary of the commissions determination with respect to the provision of teletext. First, the commission determined that teletext was expected to provide services that were ancillary to the regular broadcast audio-visual program service of television stations. As an ancillary activity, the commission believed teletext would not be required to further or promote a station's performance with respect to its public service obligation as it related to programming.[225]

Second, it concluded, as it had proposed in its original Notice, that, as a matter of law, the political broadcasting requirements in Section 312(a)(7) and 315 of the Act should not apply to teletext.[226] Section 312(a)(7) requires licensees to "allow reasonable access for the use of a broadcasting station by a legally qualified candidate for Federal elective office on behalf of his candidacy." 47 U.S.C. Sec. 312(1)(7). But the commission determined there was no legal requirement that licensees grant federal candidates access to their teletext service offerings.[227]

It also concluded that Section 315 was not applicable to teletext offerings. This was based on its finding that teletext was not a medium by which a candidate could make a personal appearance. Assuming a fundamental dissimilarity between teletext and the types of broadcast "uses" envisioned by Congress in Section 315, it also concluded that the equal opportunities requirement need not be applied to teletext services.[228]

Nested in this technically grounded ruling was, without question, its most significant determination. It held that "in 1959, Congress amended Section 315(1) to exclude certain types of news programming from the 'equal opportunities' requirement, and, in doing so, added language recognizing the Commission's Fairness Doctrine policy."[229] It continues by saying, "in our view, Congress' purpose in adding this language was solely to ratify the Commission's then-existing policy concerning application of the Fairness Doctrine to news broadcasts."[230]

This single statement, drawn on in a later court case, would serve as the basis for the commission's 1987 decision to relieve itself from its obligation to enforce the fairness doctrine. Now, however, the commission used it as a means of extending its determination that "the 1959 legislative enactment concerning the Fairness Doctrine in

Section 315 does not mandate extension of the Fairness Doctrine to new services like teletext, which did not even exist at the time when Congress acted. Rather, any determination concerning this question is one which has been entrusted to our sound judgment and discretion in the first instance."[231]

In her concurring statement, commissioner Anne Jones raised the point made above about the true nature of markets and competition. For her, there was an inconsistency raised in the commission's teletext decision. She said, "as broadcast technology evolves, new uses of broadcast spectrum become possible,"[232] and teletext was just one example for her. Since existing broadcast licensees were already authorized as such to use spectrum, they had immediate access to the frequencies necessary to offer teletext. She believed it was entirely appropriate for the commission to ask whether existing broadcast licensees necessarily had an implied exclusive franchise to offer new services on their assigned frequencies. She concluded:

> If the Commission desires to establish new markets in communications services made possible by advancing technology, it should consider the competitive implications of an incumbent licensee's automatic access to the spectrum. To enable new participants to enter the market for new communications services, the Commission may wish to redefine the nature of the implicit "spectrum rights" granted to broadcast licensees.[233]

This idea was also reflected in FCC commissioner Joseph R. Fogarty's last major speech as a member of the commission. He called for major changes in approaches to several facets of telecommunications regulation--and deregulation. Addressing a conference on the new telecommunication's marketplace in San Francisco, in May, 1983, Fogarty said that unless the emerging competition was full and fair for all entities, "there will occur in even greater magnitude such marketplace distortions as uneconomic bypass or service disruptions which, in turn, will deprive the American public of the supposed benefits of competition."[234]

At its meeting the last week of June, the commission, in a unanimous 5-0 vote (with commissioner Henry Rivera concurring) launched a rulemaking proposing to deregulate commercial television as it already had deregulated radio.[235] The commission, also by a unanimous vote, launched a further notice of proposed rulemaking aimed at coming up with a revised logging requirement for commercial broadcasters. These rulemakings were to consider eliminating most programming, commercialization, ascertainment and program log "burdens" from commercial TV broadcasters.[236]

By congressional mandate, the FCC would have a maximum of five commissioners starting Friday, July 1. Actually there were only four since terms of commissioners Fogarty and Sharp expired Thursday, June 30, and the vacancy created by the resignation of Anne Jones had not been filled.

The Mutual Broadcasting System announced on Monday, July 18, 1983, it would launch a print advertising campaign advocating repeal of the fairness doctrine. The campaign would feature full-page ads in *Atlantic Monthly, Forbes, Nation's Business* and *Newsweek,* and would be accompanied by spots on the Mutual Radio Network.[237] According to Mutual president and chief executive officer, Martin Rubenstein, the ads would attempt "to begin the process of educating Congress and the electorate about the real meaning of the fairness doctrine and the need for its repeal." The copy read:

> The First Amendment guarantees the rights of free speech and freedom of the press which magazines and newspapers enjoy. But these constitutional rights are effectively denied to radio and television by federal regulations that govern the content of news broadcasters.
>
> The "Fairness Doctrine," which embodies several regulations, is a good case in point. It looks good in theory since it proposes "equal opportunity" for and "reasonable access" to opposing viewpoints. In practice, it doesn't work. Stations often choose to remain silent on many important issues for fear of opening a Pandora's box of competing claims for airtime. The result is that viewpoints which could contribute to public knowledge and debate go unheard.
>
> According to a recent Roper poll, 82% of Americans now get their news primarily from the broadcast media. For this majority, the press is radio and TV. But these media are not protected by the First Amendment. Could this have been the intent of our founding fathers? We don't think so.
>
> When the primary news source for a majority of citizens is denied its First Amendment rights, it's time we all became alarmed. At the Mutual Broadcasting System we think it's time to give radio and television the same First Amendment protections that newspapers and

magazines have enjoyed since 1791. Congress should repeal the so-called "Fairness Doctrine" in the name of fairness.[238]

The appointment of James C. McKinney, FCC Private Radio bureau chief, to be Mass Media bureau chief the last week of July, came as a surprise to the broadcast industry. McKinney replaced Laurence Harris. Most industry observers had thought that the Mass Media Bureau's deputy chief, Jeff Bauman, would get the appointment.[239] McKinney's appointment may have initially concerned the broadcasters, but their concerns were to be groundless. His regulatory philosophy he said were the same as Fowler's. He said he believed the electronic media should be "following the print model."[240]

Also, by the end of July most observers believed that White House personnel aide Dennis Patrick would be appointed to fifth seat on the FCC.[241]

During the second week of August, at its only scheduled meeting of the month, the commission pushed back its deadline for comments on its proposal to repeal its personal attack and political editorializing rules. It moved the deadline from August 22 until Sept. 5. It also moved its deadline for reply comments to September 30.[242]

The FCC's proposal to re-examine its application of the fairness doctrine and equal time rules to cable television[243] was given significant coverage in the broadcast trade press. Cable operators were for getting rid of those obligations, but public interest groups wanted them applied.[244]

But more significant than whether the rules applied to cable was the broader question the FCC's notice raised. That is, should the fairness obligations be scrapped altogether?[245] In a September 5, 1983, editorial, *Broadcasting* drew extensively on the National Cable Television legal theory that the fairness doctrine lacked codification. NCTA hoped this would liberate cable operators from the fairness doctrine. As the editorial said, "It may not have been the NCTA's intention, but if the theory were accepted by the FCC and upheld by the courts, it conceivably could extricate broadcasters from the same bondage."[246]

In another editorial on September 19, 1983, *Broadcasting* again stressed NCTA's argument on the lack of codification of the fairness doctrine. Though *Broadcasting* did not advocate relieving cable of any obligation, it did argue for its own benefit that:

There can be little question that the FCC has the power to take back it personal attack and political editorializing rules, and the history of both has given it every reason to do so. The rules have been applied with conflicting results by different compositions of the FCC. Both are excessive applications of the fairness doctrine, and both inhibit journalistic enterprise.[247]

At a two-day conference the last week of September in Washington, titled "Campaign '84: Advertising and Programming Obligations of the Electronic Media," Milton Gross, head of the FCC's Complaints divisions said "90% of our election complaints are handled and disposed of by telephone." In 1980 Gross said his staff issued 12 rules in two days, but that in 1982 they issued only two decisions in a 60-day period.[248]

At the same panel, Daniel Armstrong, FCC associate general counsel, whose office represented the FCC in litigation on political fairness questions, encouraged parties in litigation to consider filing with the U.S. Court of Appeals, District of Columbia. Armstrong said the appeals court "is very receptive to expedited rulings" and also had developed a certain "expertise on this type of litigation.[249] He was referring to the courts' decision the week before in *Democratic National Committee v. CBS*,[250] which described a successful fairness doctrine complaint as "a rare creature."

Broadcasting gave the DNC case extensive coverage. In this case, the Court affirmed an FCC action rejecting a Democratic National Committee fairness complaint against CBS and NBC. The complaint was based on the networks' airing in the fall of 1981 of a series of 30-second spots, sponsored by the Republican National Committee, supporting President Reagan's economic program.[251]

The commission had held that the Democrats had not made the *prima facie* case that would cause it to investigate the complaint. It said the Democrats had not offered evidence to indicate the networks' overall programming was "unreasonably imbalanced," or that the public had been left "uninformed" on the issue. The fairness doctrine does not require equal time, the court said, adding, "Reasonableness was the guidepost that the commission correctly used in reaching its decision regarding DNC's complaint."[252]

While affirming the commission's rejection of the DNC complaint, the court was constrained to say a word in behalf of the fairness doctrine, which, it said, remained "a vital aspect" of the broadcasting regime, despite the "formidable obstacles" facing the filer of a fairness complaint.[253] The court quoted statistics for fairness complaints filed between 1973 and 1976 that indicated that the average complainant had about a one-in-1,000 chance of seeing the commission punish a station.[254] The court also said it felt constrained in its decision because of what it called a "gratuitous comment" in the commission opinion which could be read as suggesting it would be "futile" to challenge broadcasters on fairness grounds in cases like that presented by the DNC complaint.[255]

Promised legislation to repeal equal time and fairness doctrine, and lift other Communications Act limits on TV and radio, was introduced October 3, 1983, by Senator Packwood.[256] This spelled the official end to Packwood's push for a constitutional amendment. In a floor statement, Packwood said the proposal (S-1917), called "Freedom of Expression Act," would "remove the stigma of second class citizenship for broadcasters." Packwood blamed his original constitutional amendment idea's failure on lack of support from the broadcast and the print media.[257] But his measure now drew the quick support from the NAB, whose Executive Committee passed resolution of endorsement at its October 5 monthly meeting. The resolution urged members to press for its enactment.[258]

On Friday, October 14, 1983, Ronald Reagan announced his intention to nominate Dennis R. Patrick to the FCC for the unexpired term of 7 years from July 1, 1978. He would succeed Anne P. Jones.[259] Patrick had earned his undergraduate degree from Occidental College, and his law degree from the University of California at Los Angeles School of Law (J.D., 1976). Between 1976 and 1981, Patrick practiced law with the law offices of Adams, Duque & Hazeltine in Los Angeles, California. Since December of 1981 he had served as Associate Director of Presidential Personnel at the White House where he was responsible for legal and regulatory agencies.[260]

At 32, Patrick would be one of the youngest commissioners ever. Reaction to Patricks' nomination varied. FCC chairman Mark Fowler said, "He's certainly an excellent choice."[261] But Sam Simon, executive director of TRAC, had his doubts. He said of Patrick: "As far as I can tell, he's a clone of the Reagan administration philosophy. I'd be surprised if he had any intention of enforcing the 1934 Communications Act, but if he does ... I'll be glad to work with him."[262]

The commission refused to grant a declaratory ruling aimed at preventing broadcasters from having to provide free time to the opponents of supporters of candidates to whom the broadcaster have sold time for political ads.[263]   This action came at a commission meeting the second week of November.   Denial of this declaratory ruling reaffirmed both the commission's Cullman doctrine, and its Zapple doctrine.   The Cullman doctrine[264] holds that a broadcaster, under the fairness doctrine, have to air contrasting views, even if a broadcaster cannot find someone willing to pay for the airing.   The FCC's Zapple doctrine,[265] which applies only during campaign periods, holds that broadcasters who sell broadcast time to the supporters on one major-party candidate only have to offer to sell comparable amounts of time to that candidate's major-party opponents in a similar time-slot.

Following the commission's ruling, Fowler said he thought the broadcasters in their request for the declaratory ruling, were more concerned about having to give away some free time than they were about first amendment issues.[266]   It seems more than curious that he may have just then come to that conclusion.   It never bothered him enough though to flavor his future determinations.

The Senate adjourned in November until January, 1984.   It did so without holding a confirmation hearing for White House aide Dennis Patrick.   *Television Digest* reported that Senator Goldwater (R-Arizona), chairman of the Communications Subcommittee, had put a hold on the confirmation because he was seeking a judicial appointment for a friend.[267]

The White House exercised its option to make interim appointments on November 30.   Former White House aide Dennis Patrick was sworn in as the FCC's fifth member on December 2, after receiving a recess appointment which did not require Senate action.[268] Most expected Patrick would support Fowler's positions.   He became the third Republican member of the commission along with Fowler and Dawson.

Notes

1981

[1]"An acid test for the fairness doctrine." Joe S. Maynor. *TV Guide*. November 15, 1980. v.28. pp.16-8,20. At p.20.

[2]"Ways Reagan will curb the regulators." *U.S. News & World Report*. December 15, 1980. v.89. pp.34-5. At p.34.

[3]Ibid.

[4]Ibid.

[5]"Telecommunications." Maurice Barnfather. *Forbes*. January 5, 1981. v.127. pp.225-6. At p.225.

[6]Ibid.

[7]"Lee chairman for awhile, then Fowler: White House transition team." *Television Digest*. January 19, 1981. 21:3. pp.1-2. At p.1.

[8]Ibid., at p.2.

[9]Ibid.

[10]"Who's who in the administration." *Washington Monthly*. February, 1981. v.12. pp.53-5. At p.55.

[11]"Changing the rules." David Alpern and Jerry Buckley. *Newsweek*. March 2, 1981. v.97. pp.30-1. At p.30.

[12]Ibid.

[13]Ibid.

[14]Ibid., at p.31.

[15]Ibid.

[16]"Fowler is official: White House announced Friday." *Television Digest*. March 9, 1981. 21:11. p.3.

[17]"Nomination of Mark S. Fowler to be a member of the Federal Communications Commission, and designation as chairman." Ronald Reagan. *Public Papers of the Presidents: Ronald Reagan: 1981*. U.S. Government Printing Office. Washington: 1983. March 13, 1981. p.23.

[18]"Fowler is official: White House announced Friday." *Television Digest*. March 9, 1981. 21:11. p.3.

[19]"Lee control now official." *Television Digest*. March 9, 1981. 21:11. p.6.

[20]Ibid.

[21]"Nomination of Mary Ann Weyforth Dawson to be a commissioner of the Federal Communications Commission." Ronald Reagan. *Public Papers of the Presidents: Ronald Reagan: 1981*. U.S. Government Printing Office. Washington: 1983. April 6, 1981. p.334.

[22]"Rivera nomination on way." *Television Digest.* April 27, 1981. 21:17. p.1.

[23]Hearings Before the Committee on Commerce, Science, and Transportation, U.S.Senate, 97th Congress, 1st Session. Nominations of Mark S. Fowler, to be chairman; and Mary Ann Weyforth Dawson, to be a commissioner, Federal Communications Commission. May 1 and May 21, 1981. Serial No. 97-46. At p.1.

[24]Ibid.

[25]Ibid.

[26]Brenner, Daniel. "Policy-making at the Fowler FCC: How speeches figured in." *Hastings Journal of Communications and Entertainment Law.* 10:2. Winter 1988. pp.539-554. At p.553.

[27]Hearings Before the Committee on Commerce, Science, and Transportation. U.S. Senate, 97th Congress, 1st Session. Nominations of Mark S. Fowler, to be chairman; and Mary Ann Weyforth Dawson, to be a commissioner, Federal Communications Commission. May 1 and May 21, 1981. Serial No. 97-46. At p.4.

[28]Ibid.

[29]Ibid., at p.5.

[30]Ibid., at p.11.

[31]Hearing Before the Committee on Commerce, Science, and Transportation, U.S. Senate, 97th Congress, 1st Session. On S. 821, A Bill to Provide for Authorization of Appropriations for the Federal Communications Commission, May 1, 1981, Serial No. 97-34. At p.18+.

[32]Ibid., at p.19.

[33]Ibid.

[34]Ibid., at p.20.

[35]Hearings Before the Committee on Commerce, Science, and Transportation, U.S. Senate, 97th Congress, 1st Session. Nominations of Mark S. Fowler, to be chairman; and Mary Ann Weyforth Dawson, to be a commissioner, Federal Communications Commission. May 1 and May 21, 1981. Serial No. 97-46. At p.17.

[36]Ibid., at p.18.

[37]Ibid.

[38]"Can Reagan rope the regulators?" Ann M. Reilly. *Dun's Review.* May, 1981. v.117. p.40(6). At p.48.

[39]Ibid.

[40]"Fowler moves in." *Television Digest.* May 21, 1981. 21:21. p.7.

[41]Ibid.

[42]Ibid.

[43]"The FCC: On a new wavelength." *Business Week.* May 25, 1981. p.172.

[44]Ibid.

[45]Ibid.

[46]"Nomination of Henry M. Rivera to be a member of the Federal Communications Commission." Ronald Reagan. *Public Papers of the Presidents: Ronald Reagan: 1981*. U.S. Government Printing Office. Washington: 1983. June 5, 1981. p.492.

[47]"Nomination of James Henry Quello to be a member of the Federal Communications Commission." Ronald Reagan. *Public Papers of the Presidents: Ronald Reagan: 1981*. U.S. Government Printing Office. Washington: 1983. June 5, 1981. p.492.

[48]Ibid.

[49]"Fowler imprint on FCC due in fall." *Television Digest*. July 27, 1981. 21:30. p.3.

[50]Ibid.

[51]Hearing Before the Committee on Commerce, Science, and Transportation, U.S. Senate, 97th Congress, 1st Session. Nominations of James H. Quello and Henry M. Rivera, to be commissioners, Federal Communications Commission. July 22, 1981. Serial No. 97-50. At p.3.

[52]Ibid.

[53]Ibid., at p.4.

[54]Ibid., at pp.5-6.

[55]Ibid., at p.7.

[56]Ibid., at p.14.

[57]"Fowler - no more First Amendment encroachments." *Television Digest*. August 24, 1981. 21:34. p.2.

[58]Ibid.

[59]Ibid.

[60]Ibid.

[61]"Fowler on Rivera." *Television Digest*. August 24, 1981. 21:34. p.5.

[62]See: Hearing Before the Committee on Energy and Commerce, Subcommittee on Telecommunications, Consumer Protection, and Finance, U.S. House of Representatives, 97th Congress, 1st Session. Broadcast Reform Proposals. December 9, 1981.

[63]"Fowler FCC full speed ahead on 'unregulation'." *Television Digest*. September 21, 1981. 21:38. pp.1-3. At p.1.

[64]Ibid., at p.2.

[65]Ibid.

[66]Ibid.

[67]Ibid.

[68]Ibid.

[69]Ibid.

[70]Ibid., at p.3.

[71]Ibid.

[72]"Fowler FCC redefining public interest." *Television Digest.* September 28, 1981. 21:39. p.3.

[73]Ibid.

[74]Ibid.

[75]Notice of Proposed Rule Making in BC Docket 81-741. 46 FR 60851. October 22, 1981.

[76]Remarks Before the American Association of Advertising Agencies, Inc. Mark Fowler. October 26, 1981. Washington, DC. In "The Federal Communications Commission 1981-1987: What the chairman said." *Hastings COMM/ENT Law Journal.* Winter 1988. Vol 10. pp.409-500. At p.445.

[77]Ibid.

[78]"Dereg bill introduced." *Television Digest.* October 26, 1981. 21:43. p.3.

[79]Hearing Before the Committee on Energy and Commerce, Subcommittee on Telecommunications, Consumer Protection, and Finance, U.S. House of Representatives, 97th Congress, 1st Session. Broadcast Reform Proposals. December 9, 1981. Serial No. 97-76. pp.77-91.

[80]"Don't deregulate TV, House report urges." *Television Digest.* November 9, 1981. 21:42. pp.1-2. At p.1.

[81]"Watch political regulations - Hollings." *Television Digest.* December 21, 1981. 21:46. p.6.

[82]Pub. L. No. 97-35, 95 Stat. 357 (1981).

1982

[83]"Larry Harris: FCC's new super-bureau chief." *Broadcasting.* January 11, 1982. v.102. pp.30-1. At p.30.

[84]Ibid.

[85]"Getting the government out of programming: FCC chief calls it 'unregulation'." Mark S. Fowler. *Variety.* January 13, 1982. v.305. pp.145,182. At p.182.

[86]"The NAB salutes Fowler power." Vincent Wasilewski (President, NAB). *Variety.* January 13, 1982. v.305. pp.145,183.

[87]Ibid., at p.145.

[88]Ibid., at p.183.

[89]"4A's press end of fairness." *Back Stage.* January 15, 1982. v.23. pp.31-2.

[90]Address Before the National Religious Broadcasters. February 9, 1982. In "The Federal Communications Commission 1981-1987: What the

chairman said." *Hastings COMM/ENT Law Journal*. Winter 1988. Vol 10. pp.409-500. At p.445.

[91]Remarks Before the Thomas Jefferson Awards Dinner. February 19, 1982. Ibid., at p.437.

[92]Ibid.

[93]"Within the inner circle: A review of the FCC members." Victor Block. *Telephony*. January 18, 1982. v.202. pp.58-60,65-6. At p.58.

[94]Ibid., at p.65.

[95]Ibid.

[96]Ibid., at p.66.

[97]Ibid.

[98]Ibid.

[99]"Dilemma for the Fowler FCC: Yesterday's marketplace, or tomorrow's?" *Broadcasting*. February 8, 1982. v.102. pp.36-38,42. At p.42.

[100]"Within the inner circle: A review of the FCC members." Victor Block. *Telephony*. January 18, 1982. v.202. pp.58-60,65-6. At p.66.

[101]"Dilemma for the Fowler FCC: Yesterday's marketplace, or tomorrow's?" *Broadcasting*. February 8, 1982. v.102. pp.36-38,42. At p.36.

[102]Ibid., at p.37.

[103]"Door is open, FCC's Harris tells lawyers." *Broadcasting*. January 25, 1982. v.102. p.68.

[104]"Fairness, equal time to general counsel?" *Television Digest*. February 22, 1982. 22:8. pp.1-2. At p.1.

[105]Ibid., at p.2.

[106]"Law & Regulation: Fogarty wants fairness branch to stay put." *Broadcasting*. March 1, 1982. v.102. p.94.

[107]Ibid.

[108]Ibid.

[109]Ibid.

[110]"Broyhill's dereg package." *Television Digest*. March 1, 1982. v.22. p.4.

[111]Ibid.

[112]"Fowler - Familiar theme." *Television Digest*. March 22, 1982. 22:12. p.4.

[113]"Market forces will be deciding who gets piece of video market." by Mark S. Fowler. *Communications News*. April, 1982. v.19. pp.58-9.

[114]Ibid., at p.58.

[115]Ibid.

[116]Address Before National Association of Broadcasters. April 7, 1982. Dallas, Texas. In "The Federal Communications Commission 1981-

1987: What the chairman said." *Hastings COMM/ENT Law Journal*. Winter 1988. Vol 10. pp.409-500. At pp.438-41.

[117]"FCC commissioners on line." *Television Digest*. April 12, 1982. v.22. p.6.

[118]Ibid.

[119]Ibid.

[120]Ibid.

[121]"Latest plan to loosen the reins on broadcasting." *U.S. News & World Report*. April 12, 1982. v.92. pp.43-4. At p.43.

[122]"Reagan enters Sharp-Weatherly fight." *Television Digest*. April 19, 1982. 22:16. p.1.

[123]"Showdown." (editorial) *Broadcasting*. April 19, 1982. v.102. p.98.

[124]Ibid.

[125]"Weiker's regulation worry." *Television Digest*. April 26, 1982. 22:17. p.5.

[126]"Nomination of Stephen A. Sharp to be a member of the Federal Communications Commission." Ronald Reagan. *Public Papers of the Presidents: Ronald Reagan: 1982*. U.S. Government Printing Office. Washington: 1984. May 19, 1982. pp.654-5.

[127]"Sharp nomination runs into snag." *Broadcasting*. May 24, 1982. v.102. pp.31-2. At p.31.

[128]Ibid.

[129]"Fewer FCC commissioners?" *Television Digest*. May 17, 1982. 22:20. p.5.

[130]"Sparks fly: President Reagan nominates Sharp to serve on FCC." Victor Block. *Telephony*. May 31, 1982. v.202. p.12.

[131]"Fowler's first year in review." *Broadcasting*. May 24, 1982. v.102. pp.47-8. At p.47.

[132]Ibid.

[133]Ibid., at pp.47-8.

[134]Ibid., at p.48.

[135]FCC Authorization, Hearing Before the Subcommittee on Communications of the Committee on Commerce, Science, and Transportation, U.S.Senate, 98th Congress, 1st Session. On S.607 To Amend the Communications Act of 1934, March 9, 1983, Serial No. 98-14.

[136]*CBS, Inc. V. Democratic National Committee*, 412 U.S. 94 (1973).

[137]Remarks Before the First Amendment Congress, May 20, 1982. Leesburg, Virginia. In "The Federal Communications Commission 1981-1987: What the chairman said." *Hastings COMM/ENT Law Journal*. Winter 1988. Vol 10. pp.409-500. At p.460.

[138]Hearing Before the Subcommittee on Telecommunications, Consumer Protection, and Finance of the Committee on Energy and Commerce, U.S. House of Representatives, 97th Congress, 1st Session. On H.R. 5008. Communications Technical Amendments Act of 1981. Serial No. 97-80. November 19, 1981.

See also: Hearing Before the Subcommittee on Telecommunications, Consumer Protection, and Finance of the Committee on Energy and Commerce, U.S. House of Representatives, 97th Congress, 2nd Session. On H.R. 4726, H.R. 5252, H.R. 5584, H.R. 5585, H.R. 5752. Broadcast Regulation Reform Proposals. Serial No. 97-140. May 6, 1982.

[139]"House committee okays FCC bill." *Television Digest*. June 7, 1982. 22:22. p.4.

[140]"Commerce committee OK's FCC lottery." *Broadcasting*. June 7, 1982. v.102. p.54.

[141]Ibid.

[142]"Tea leaves favor change in FCC position on multiple ownership." *Broadcasting*. July 5, 1982. v.103. pp.27-8. At p.28.

[143]Ibid.

[144]Fowler, Mark, and D. Brenner. "A marketplace approach to broadcast regulation." Reprinted in E. Wartella *et al.*, ed. *Mass Communication Review Yearbook 4* (Beverly Hills: Sage): pp.645-95. Originally 60 *Texas Law Review* 207 (1982), pp.207-57.

[145]"Do broadcasters really want total freedom?" *Television Digest*. July 12, 1982. 22:28. pp.2-3. At p.3.

[146]"Seven to five." *Broadcasting*. July 19, 1982. v.103. p.36.

[147]Ibid.

[148]"Free speech for electronic media." *Television Digest*. August 2, 1982. 22:31. p.3.

[149]"FCC meeting light on broadcast." *Television Digest*. August 2, 1982. 22:31. p.4.

[150]"Senate votes to cut FCC to 5 commissioners." *Broadcasting*. August 9, 1982. v.103. pp.25-6. At p.26.

[151]"Congress approves cut of 2 FCC commissioners." *Television Digest*. August 23, 1982. 22:34. pp.1-2. At p.1.

[152]Hearing Before the Subcommittee on Telecommunications, Consumer Protection, and Finance of the Committee on Energy and Commerce, U.S. House of Representatives, 97th Congress, 1st Session. On H.R. 5008. Communications Technical Amendments Act of 1981. Serial No. 97-80. November 19, 1981.

See also: Hearing Before the Subcommittee on Telecommunications, Consumer Protection, and Finance of the Committee on Energy and Commerce, U.S. House of

Representatives, 97th Congress, 2nd Session. On H.R. 4726, H.R. 5252, H.R. 5584, H.R. 5585, H.R. 5752. Broadcast Regulation Reform Proposals. Serial No. 97-140. May 6, 1982.

[153]"Congress approves cut of 2 FCC commissioners." *Television Digest*. August 23, 1982. 22:34. pp.1-2. At p.1.

[154]Address Before the National Radio Broadcasters Association. September 13, 1982. Reno, Nevada. In "The Federal Communications Commission 1981-1987: What the chairman said." *Hastings COMM/ENT Law Journal*. Winter 1988. Vol 10. pp.409-500. At pp.438-31,451-2.

[155]Ibid., at p.452.

[156]"FCC wraps it all up." *Broadcasting*. September 20, 1982. v.103. pp.52-3. At p.52.

[157]Ibid.

[158]"FCC's new Mass Media Bureau." *Television Digest*. September 20, 1982. 22:38. p.2.

[159]Nomination-FCC, Hearing Before the Committee n Commerce, Science, and Transportation, U.S.Senate, 97th Congress, 2nd Session. On Stephen A. Sharp, to be a Commissioner, Federal Communications Commission, September 22, 1982, Serial No. 97-131.

[160]Ibid., at p.3.

[161]Ibid., at p.41.

[162]Ibid., at pp.13-14.

[163]Ibid.

[164]"Fowler stresses fee trade-off for deregulation." *Broadcasting*. September 27, 1982. v.103. pp.33-4.

[165]Ibid., at p.33.

[166]Ibid.

[167]Ibid., at p.34.

[168]Freedom of Expression. Hearings Before the Committee on Commerce, Science, and Transportation, U.S. Senate, 97th Congress, 2nd Session. On Freedom of Expression, September 28, 30, and November 19, 1982, Serial No. 97-139.

[169]Address Before the Radio Television News Directors Association: "Full First Amendment Rights for Broadcasters? Yes!". October 1, 1982. Las Vegas, Nevada. In "The Federal Communications Commission 1981-1987: What the chairman said." *Hastings COMM/ENT Law Journal*. Winter 1988. Vol 10. pp.409-500. At pp.441-2,449-51.

[170]Ibid., at 449.

[171]Ibid.

[172]Ibid.

[173]"Free the broadcasting 10,000: A marketplace approach to broadcasting." Mark S. Fowler. *Vital Speeches of the Day*, December 1,

1982. Delivered before the North Carolina Association of Broadcasters, Raleigh, North Carolina, October 25, 1982. pp.104-7.

[174]Ibid., at p.105.

[175]Ibid., at p.106.

[176]Ibid.

[177]"No failure to communicate: FCC chairman's message is loud and clear." Thomas G. Donlan. *Barron's*. November 15, 1982. v.62. pp.28-9,33,35.

[178]Ibid., at p.29.

[179]Ibid., at p.33.

[180]Ibid., at pp.33,35.

[181]Ibid., at p.35.

[182]"Membership of federal regulatory agencies, 1982: Federal Communications Commission." *Congressional Quarterly Almanac*. 1982. p.20A-24A. At p.20A.

1983

[183]"Another unregulator in key FCC role." *Broadcasting*. January 10, 1983. v.104. p.36.

[184]Ibid.

[185]Ibid.

[186]Ibid.

[187]*American Security Council Education Foundation v. FCC*, 607 F.2d 438 (D.C. Cir. 1979), cert. denied, 444 U.S. 1013 (1980).

[188]"Personals." *Television Digest*. January 3, 1983. 23:1. p.8.

[189]"Fein airs views at FCBA." *Television Digest*. January 24, 1983. 23:4. p.6.

[190]Ibid.

[191]Ibid.

[192]S.22, 98th Congress, 1st Session (1983).

[193]"Persistent Proxmire." *Broadcasting*. January 17, 1983. v.104. p.80.

[194]Oversight Hearing Before the Subcommittee on Telecommunications, Consumer Protection, and Finance of the Committee on Energy and Commerce, U.S. House of Representatives, 97th Congress, 2nd Session. Broadcast, Mass Media, and Common Carrier Issues. Serial No. 97-185. December 1, 1982. At pp. 212-242.

[195]Ibid., at p.232.

[196]Ibid., at p.234.

[197]FCC Authorization, Hearing Before the Subcommittee on Communications of the Committee on Commerce, Science, and Transportation, U.S. Senate, 98th Congress, 1st Session. On S.607 to

Amend the Communications Act of 1934, March 9, 1983, Serial No. 98-14. At p.4.

[198]Ibid.

[199]Ibid., at pp.4-11.

[200]"ANPA committee urges repeal of fairness doctrine." *Editor & Publisher*. March 19, 1983. v.116. p.7.

[201]"Anne P. Jones calls it quits after 15 years." *Broadcasting*. April 11, 1983. v.104. pp.33-4. At p.33.

[202]"Fowler outlines brave new world available to broadcasters." *Broadcasting*. April 18, 1983. v.104. pp.41-2. At p.41.

[203]Ibid., at pp.41-2.

[204]Ibid., at p.41.

[205]"NAB's one-issue convention--freedom without fees." *Television Digest*. April 18, 1983. 23:16. pp.1-4. At p.1.

[206]Ibid.

[207]Ibid., at p.2.

[208]Hearing Before the Subcommittee on Telecommunications, Consumer Protection, and Finance of the Committee on Energy and Commerce, U.S. House of Representatives, 98th Congress, 1st Session. On H.R. 2755. FCC Authorization Legislation--Oversight. Serial No. 98-25. April 19, 1983.

> See also: Hearing Before the Subcommittee on Telecommunications, Consumer Protection, and Finance of the Committee on Energy and Commerce, U.S. House of Representatives, 98th Congress. 1st Session. Broadcast Regulation: Quantifying the Public Interest Standard. Serial No. 98-61. May 24, 1983.

> And: Hearing Before the Subcommittee on Telecommunications, Consumer Protection, and Finance of the Committee on Energy and Commerce, U.S. House of Representatives, 98th Congress, 1st Session. Broadcast Regulation Reform. Serial No. 98-99. August 4, and October 6, 1983.

[209]Ibid., at p.90.

[210]Ibid., at p.69.

[211]Ibid., at p.49.

[212]"FCC Commissioner Dawson sounded alarm against threats to First Amendment." *Television Digest*. April 25, 1983. 23:17. p.6.

[213]Ibid.

[214]"Sharp doesn't want Jones' FCC seat." (newest FCC commissioner Stephen Sharp and resigned Anne Jones) *Television Digest*. May 2, 1983. 23:18. pp.1-2. At p.1.

[215]"Fowler's video games: free speech, free markets, and free rides at the FCC." Marc Granetz. *The New Republic*. May 2, 1983. v.188. pp.15-8. At p.18.

[216]Ibid.

[217]Notice of Inquiry. Repeal or Modification of Personal Attack and Political Editorial Rules, 48 Fed. Reg. 28295 (June 21, 1983).

The personal attack rule, found in Section 73.1920 of the Commission's Rules, provides that when, during the presentation of controversial issues of public importance, an attack is made upon the honest, character, integrity or like personal qualities of an identified person or group, the licensee must notify the person or group attacked and offer a reasonable opportunity to respond.

The political editorial rule, found in Section 73.1930 of the Commission's Rules, provides that when a licensee endorses or opposes a legally qualified candidate in an editorial, the licensee must notify the other qualified candidates or the candidate opposed in the editorial of the broadcast and offer a reasonable opportunity to respond.

[218]"FCC eyes fairness doctrine change." *Television Digest*. May 16, 1983. 23:20. p.6.

[219]Ibid.

[220]Ibid.

[221]Ibid.

[222]Ibid.

[223]"Amendment to the Commission's Rules to Authorize the Transmission of Teletext by TV Stations." 48 Fed. Reg., no.114, Monday, June 13, 1983, pp.27054-72. 47 CFR Parts 2, 73, and 74. [BC Docket No. 81-741; FCC 83-120; RM-3727; RM-3876]

[224]Ibid., at p.27054.

[225]Ibid., at p.27061.

[226]Ibid.

[227]Ibid.

[228]Ibid.

[229]Ibid.

[230]Ibid.

[231]Ibid.

[232]Ibid., at p.27071.

[233]Ibid.

[234]"Fogarty reviews industry past and future changes." *Telephony*. July 11, 1983. v.205. pp.16,18. At p.16.

[235]Report and Order in MM Docket, No. 83-670 (Deregulation of Television), 98 FCC 2d 1076, recon. denied, 104 FCC 2d 357 (1986). Also see: Report and Order in BC Docket, No. 79-219 (Deregulation of Radio), 84 FCC 2d 968, recon. denied, 87 FCC 2d 797 (1981); and Report and Order in MM Docket No. 84-19, FCC 84-156 (released May 9, 1984), 55 RR 2d 1389 (1984), recon. denied, FCC 85-225 (released May 8, 1985) (Elimination of Regional Concentration Rule).

[236]Report and Order, MM Docket No. 83-670, 55 RR 2d 1005 (1983). In eliminating the programming guidelines, the commission noted that there had been an increasing amount of informational and total nonentertainment programming and that commercial television stations had been meeting the demand for such programming.

[237]"Mutual goes after fairness doctrine." *Broadcasting*. July 25, 1983. v.105. pp.85-6. At p.85.

[238]Ibid., at p.86.

[239]"James McKinney: Fowler's hand-picked mover and shaker for the Mass Media Bureau." *Broadcasting*. August 1, 1983. v.105. pp.41,44. At p.41.

[240]Ibid., at p.44.

[241]"'Fowler rule' on financial interest helps networks." *Television Digest*. August 1, 1983. 23:31. pp.1-2. At p.2.

[242]"Postponed." *Broadcasting*. August 15, 1983. v.105. p.68.

[243]Report and Order in General Docket No. 83-1009, FCC 84-350, 49 Fed. Reg. 31877 (August 9, 1984), recon. granted in part, Memorandum Opinion and Order, FCC 84-638, 50 Fed. Reg. 4666 (February 1, 1985).

[244]"Back and forth on fairness." *Broadcasting*. September 5, 1983. v.105. pp.40-1.

[245]Ibid., at p.41.

[246]"The case for freedom." (editorial) *Broadcasting*. September 5, 1983. v.105. p.114.

[247]"A chance to make a difference." (editorial) *Broadcasting*. September 19, 1983. v.105. p.138.

[248]"The media: The problems and potential of political advertising." *Broadcasting*. October 3, 1983. v.105. pp.90-2,94. At p.91.

[249]Ibid.

[250]*Columbia Broadcasting System, Inc. v. Democratic National Committee*, 412 U.S. 94 (1983).

[251]"FCC upheld in fairness challenge." *Broadcasting*. October 3, 1983. v.105. pp.102-3. At p.102.

[252]Ibid., at p.103.

[253]Ibid.

[254]Ibid.

[255]Ibid.

[256]See: Freedom of Expression Act of 1983: Hearings on S.1917 Before the Committee on Commerce, Science, and Transportation, 98th Congress, 2nd Session (1984).

Packwood also requested that a staff report prepared by NTIA be printed for use by the Senate Committee on Commerce, Science, and Transportation.

See: Print and Electronic Media: The Case for First Amendment Parity Printed at the Direction of Senator Bob Packwood for the Committee on Commerce, Science, and Transportation, 98th Congress, 1st Session (1983).

This study examined whether there should be first amendment parity between the print and electronic media.

[257]"Packwood seeks Sec. 315 repeal." *Television Digest*. October 10, 1983. 23:41. p.6.

[258]Ibid.

[259]"Nomination of Dennis R. Patrick to be a member of the Federal Communications Commission." Ronald Reagan. *Public Papers of the Presidents: Ronald Reagan: 1983*. U.S. Government Printing Office. Washington: 1985. October 14, 1983. pp.1458-9.

[260]Ibid., at p.1459.

[261]"It's official." *Broadcasting*. October 17, 1983. p.27.

[262]Ibid.

[263]"Broadcasters gain greater freedom as FCC 'clarifies' Aspen rule." *Broadcasting*. November 14, 1983. v.105. p.33.

[264]*Cullman Broadcasting Co.*, 40 FCC 576 (1963).

Here the commission stated:

> where the licensee has chosen to broadcast a sponsored program which for the first time presents one side of a controversial issue, has not presented (or does not plan to present) contrasting viewpoints in other programming, and has been unable to obtain paid sponsorship for the appropriate presentation of the opposing viewpoint or viewpoints, he cannot reject a presentation otherwise suitable to the licensee--and thus leave the public uniformed--on the ground that he cannot obtain paid sponsorship for that presentation. (Ibid., at 11-12)

[265]*Nicholas Zapple*, 23 FCC 2d 707 (1970).

The Zapple doctrine requires that if supporters, or spokesmen, for one political candidate appear on a broadcast stations, supporters for opposing candidates must be afforded similar treatment. However, the doctrine only applies to major political parties during formal campaign periods and does not require the provision of free time.

[266]Ibid.

[267]"TV dereg pushed." *Television Digest*. November 28, 1983. 23:48. p.5.

[268]"Patrick gets interim FCC term." *Television Digest*. December 5, 1983. 23:49. pp.1-2. At p.1.

CHAPTER IV

THE FAIRNESS DOCTRINE UNDER REVIEW, 1984-1985

1984

Events occurring in 1984 and 1985 would prove decisive for the continued survival of the fairness doctrine. There were three particularly important events that occurred in 1984. First, the commission decided in May to open an inquiry into the doctrine's continued viability, and also assess whether the doctrine was indeed codified in law. Second, a Supreme Court case released in July gave advocates of the doctrine's abolition hope that the courts may be willing to revisit its *Red Lion* decision. And finally, in October 1984, the commission found its first and only fairness violation. These events would ensure attention stayed focused on the fairness issue.

An illustration of the close industry ties existing between the FCC, and the industries it regulates, can be seen in the move of Henry (Jeff) Baumann, former Mass Media Bureau deputy chief. Baumann had spent most of his professional career at the FCC's Broadcast Bureau. Many expected him to succeed Larry Harris in 1983 as head of the agency's Mass Media Bureau. He had joined the FCC in October 1969 right out of Dickinson Law School as an attorney in the old Complaints and Compliance Division. From there he moved to the Hearing Division, and then the Review Board. In July 1979, he was named chief of Policy and Rules division, then deputy chief of the Bureau in August 1981. Baumann had been in the forefront of broadcast deregulation at the FCC, and had received two Senior Executive awards for work in that area.[1]

But in January, 1984, he left the agency to become the NAB's senior vice-president-general counsel. He replaced Erwin Krasnow in the highly influential post. Such easy movement from one side of the fence to the other shows how hospitable the agency/industry relationship can be.

By 1984 Mimi Dawson was well established in her position. She was believed by many to be the logical choice for next chair of the commission. This was especially true prior to Dennis Patrick's arrival at the commission. She was every bit as committed to the "magic" of the marketplace as Mark Fowler, but unlike Fowler, she had an appreciation of the political process. She also had a congressional power base--especially in the form of her ex-boss, Senator Robert Packwood.

Dawson, a converted Republican, was one of the few commissioners who was neither a lawyer nor an engineer. Though she was often in agreement with Fowler, she was never his rubber stamp. She had her own agenda, and Fowler often made compromises in his own agenda to accommodate hers.

In the third week in January, Dawson called on the commission to "quickly" launch an omnibus proceeding. This omnibus proceeding would consider getting the commission out of the business of content regulation of radio and television to the fullest extent it could under Communications Act. She made this call at a dinner meeting of Federal Communications Bar Association in Washington. She had originally made this suggestion during the commission's 1983 television deregulation proceeding, but then Fowler had persuaded her it might be better to handle question elsewhere. She knew this was politically volatile ground, because "content deregulation poses fundamental questions which go to the very heart of our legislative authority, regulatory responsibility and judicial interpretation."[2]

It was unclear why she chose to pursue this action now. It could have been a move to establish her second-in-line position now that Dennis Patrick was on board. Another explanation could be because of the obvious disagreements in Congress which virtually guaranteed no significant action would be coming from it soon. She noted the differences of opinions Senator Robert Packwood, chairman of the Senate Commerce Committee, and Representative Tim Wirth, chairman of the House Telecommunications Subcommittee, had over broadcast deregulation legislation. As she said, "we may see congressional action on broadcast deregulation in limbo. In this environment, I believe it is important, even crucial, that the commission act most deliberately, most carefully when we consider an issue of this magnitude. The Commission shouldn't allow fear that courts will reverse it to sway it from action."[3]

Senator Packwood held hearings for his Freedom of Expression Act of 1983 (S-1917) on Monday, January 30, and Wednesday, February 1 and 8. As expected, most invited witnesses spoke in its favor. But there were also a number of interest groups and witnesses who spoke against it.[4]

An interesting analysis of the situation of protection broadcaster's first amendment rights was provided by William Chamberlain and Willard Rowland.[5] They explained the meaning of a resolution that was passed at the annual convention of Association for Education in Journalism and Mass Communication (AEJMC) at Oregon State University, August 9, 1983. The resolution read:

> Recognizing that the growth and convergence of technologies for the delivery of information do not change the essential nature of communications in a free society, AEJMC reaffirms that the public interest is best served where freedom from content regulation is protected from undue economic, government and social control, regardless of the means by which information is disseminated.[6]

Officially, AEJMC did not take a position on particular provisions of Packwood's Freedom of Expression Act. But Chamberlain and Rowland explained the organization's resolution, and provided a valuable elaboration of the pertinent terms surrounding the broadcast deregulation debate.

AEJMC's resolution demonstrated subtle differences from similar resolutions passed by a number of industry media organizations represented in the hearings. It noted the goal of freedom, but also some of the real world constraints that must be addressed when seeking it. For this reason elaboration of the their testimony is given extended coverage here.

For Chamberlain and Rowland the heart of AEJMC's resolution was the statement: "the public interest is best served where freedom from content regulation is protected from undue economic, government and social control regardless of the means by which information is disseminated."[7] They explained that the members of

AEJMC supported the need to enhance the free flow of information and ideas. But they also recognized the issue of free expression involved far more than the question of government intervention into media content. Many factors other than government can, and do, restrict information flow, and must be taken into consideration during the policy-making process. And policy considerations must recognize a number of factors, principally social and economic, that constrain mass media information production and dissemination.[8]

Chamberlain and Rowland identified four terms that were subject to varying meaning in the current debate over government content regulation. They were terms used by all parties, but their meanings were not equivalent. The terms were (1) freedom, (2) scarcity, (3) "chilling effect," and (4) access and diversity. Understanding these terms and their underlying assumptions was crucial to understanding the debate.

For example, freedom appeals to fundamental American values. Deregulatory advocates using the term freedom tend to focus exclusively on the problem of media restrictions posed by action of the state. But as such, this view ignores the fact that no medium, not even the American press, is truly free in any absolute sense. It is constrained by general values, beliefs, and habits inherent in the social and political system of which it is a part.[9] The American press is also imbued with certain professional and ethical standards that are the products of the ideology, social conditions, and economic factors of the period when they emerged.[10]

Chamberlain and Rowland also point out there are powerful organizational and institutional constraints at work in the operations of the press and mass media. Mass production techniques themselves limit the freedom of action by professionals working within them. It is a system that emphasizes information that can be easily acquired, rapidly prepared, and attractively packaged. Freedom as a concept is quite complex, and appropriate public policy seeking freedom in communications goes beyond simple doctrines of restriction on government.[11]

The second term Chamberlain and Rowland identify as disputed in the deregulation debate is scarcity. Proponents of broadcast deregulation argue the introduction of so many new technologies (e.g. cable, satellites, low power television, cassettes, cellular radio, personal computers, fiber optics, etc.), render the conditions of spectrum scarcity underlying original broadcasting legislation irrelevant.[12] But the difficulty of this assumption is a misinterpretation of a trend towards less scarcity as an already accomplished fact. The fact remains that these opportunities are expensive and not universally available. The use of the broadcast portion of the spectrum still requires a grant of a license. And this grant of a license remains a monopoly privilege to use a particular frequency. Chamberlain and Rowland point out that spectrum abundance exists only in a relative sense; and it should not be confused with the complete elimination of scarcity. Viewed this way, public policy consequences are more complicated than the end-of-scarcity assertions have it.[13]

The third concept identified by Chamberlain and Rowland as necessary to understand in the broadcast deregulation debate is the notion of "chilling effect." Proponents of the proposition cite anecdotal evidence and literature adduced in hearings and elsewhere.[14] While opponents to the "chilling effect" argument contend content rules have, in fact, worked to increase public access. For them, a dictum such as the fairness doctrine, can be seen "not [as] a restraint on the first Amendment--but [as] a stimulus to it."[15] Chamberlain and Rowland continue by advising that censorship is claimed by those advocating the "chilling effect" argument. But self-censorship is implicit in the very structural forms and economic bases of the media. The problem is, again, more complicated than that of government intervention in the focus, range, and adequacy of electronic media content.[16]

The final concept identified by Chamberlain and Rowland is that of access and diversity. How does one provide the most effective protection for the right of the public to receive suitable access to a variety of ideas and experiences? Those advocating broadcast deregulation assume that through deregulation, the encouragement of new technologies, and elimination of government restrictions, it is possible to create a free marketplace in electronic communication. The free marketplace will provide the conditions for open competition, which in turn lead to adequate diversity of information and expression.[17]

But, again, most of the support for this proposition is speculative. It is based upon such other problematic assumptions as the end-of-scarcity doctrine. It also ignores certain historical and continuing realities about the nature of American communications. The historical problem, as Chamberlain and Rowland perceive the situation, is there never has been a free and open marketplace in industrialized communications. The purposes, and industrial characteristics of the American mass media and telecommunications was already in place before regulation was established. It was a commercial, centralizing, mass producing, nationally syndicated ("network") pattern. Subsequent legislation and regulation largely ratified an existing structure.[18] These conditions are so well entrenched that, in spite of all the current policy efforts to introduce new technologies and competing parties, the ultimate consequences for electronic media content and services, as juxtaposed against all the expectations and promises, appear limited and disappointing.[19]

Chamberlain and Rowland point to a growing body of communication research that variously documents the problems associated with communications deregulation. Problems such as economic forces at work, which even in deregulated radio encourage considerable duplication of existing forms of service rather than distinctly different program and information forms. And the tendency in industry and policy making debate to confuse increases in numbers of channels with increases in range of content.[20]

As mentioned at the beginning of this study, changes in federal policy for common carrier, broadcasting, cable, and the entire array of new electronic communications were originally to have been considered altogether in a complex pattern of trade-offs. In this context, public service needs would not have been overlooked by Congress. But because Congress had failed to act, now separated regulatory, judicial, and legislative proceedings have been broken apart into a series of piece-meal actions. These separated proceedings tended primarily to support the needs of certain interested parties. Chamberlain and Rowland remind us that appeals to constitutional principle can mask efforts designed primarily to seek economic advantage.[21] Minimizing governmental control of mass media content is an admirable goal, but the nature of the electronic media justifies public interest considerations. This is especially true for requirements to provide programming that may not otherwise be disseminated.[22]

In what *Television Digest* called "prosecutorial style,"[23] the House Telecommunications Subcommittee questioned FCC chairman Fowler for nearly five hours on Wednesday, February 8.[24] Questioning ranged from financial interest and syndication, to children's television, to the fairness doctrine. Panel Chairman Wirth (D-Colorado) reminded Fowler, and the three other commissioners present (Dennis Patrick did not attend), that the oversight hearings were started as a way "to increase the FCC's accountability."[25] Wirth expressed his concern at what he considered to be the FCC's irresponsibility. In this case, the commission's irresponsibility in ending its children's television rulemaking without taking action.[26]

In a February 13 interview with *Broadcasting*, Senator Packwood continued to seek industry support for his Freedom of Expression Act. He explained that what his bill would do to the public interest standard. He said, "it redefines it. ... It does not repeal the terms public interest, but it leaves them with very little with which to weigh against."[27] This had become the standard ploy of deregulation proponents.

Broadcasting asked Packwood if he supported commissioner Dawson's proposed omnibus rulemaking to eliminate all content regulation that the commission was authorized to repeal. Packwood said he was "perfectly happy to have the commission go as far as it can go legally."[28] And when asked why there was less broadcast support for his original Constitutional amendment, he replied, "Some of them like the protection they are given."[29] This statement captures the true nature of the debate.

Packwood based much of his appeal for support on technological convergence. He used this particularly as a means of involving the print media in his campaign. Citing particularly teletext, he warned that, "Newspapers are using teletext, and that could put them under the jurisdiction of the FCC."[30]

The fourth week of February, the FCC put off its decision to launch a general inquiry into the fairness doctrine obligations of broadcast licensees. The item was not shelved though. *Broadcasting*, citing unnamed commission sources, said that it would be ready for action at the FCC's regularly scheduled meeting March 14.[31] The notice of inquiry had been drafted by the Office of General Counsel. It was pulled from the agenda by Fowler because it was in need of some editing, according to *Broadcasting*.[32]

During the Thursday, March 22, 1984, FCC *en banc* meeting to receive public views, the frustration of Fowler's insensitivity to public interest group concerns reached a head. Telecommunications

Research and Action Center (TRAC) Executive Director Samuel Simon, alleged that Fowler had demonstrated "clear and unalterable bias" in favor of some industries, and that his votes always are in their favor.[33]

This reaction by Simon was indicative of the increasing frustration public interest groups felt toward the commission. Simon cited a number of commission rulemakings that were imbued with Fowler's own "ideological fervor." These rulemakings included television deregulation; repeal of personal attack and political editorialization rules; elimination of regional and national station ownership limitations; repeal of fairness doctrine; and telephone access charges.[34]

Simon concluded by saying, "Your ideological bent has become a theological cause. You cannot be persuaded, you cannot be reasoned with and you should not in all fairness be permitted to continue in this charade of pretending to execute the duties of your office to faithfully uphold the law of the land." When he finished his prepared remarks, Simon and several followers walked out of the meeting.[35]

Six months after Reagan's nomination, Dennis Patrick finally received his confirmation hearing on Monday, March 26, 1984. Senator Goldwater opened the hearings by apologizing for the delay. Goldwater said:

> Mr. Patrick, I want to apologize for the long delay in having your hearing, but I will be honest with you. I was playing politics. I had been made a promise by the White House about 3-1/2 years ago, and I was just trying to see if they would keep it. They didn't, but any way, I am going to hold your hearing, and I don't think you will have any trouble.[36]

Patrick, in his opening statement, outlined his previous experience, and regulatory philosophy. He had served two years as the White House's Associate Director of Presidential Personnel for Legal and Regulatory Agencies. He said he would "approach the issues facing the Commission with an open mind." He said that the public interest could best be defined by the public itself. But then he continued by saying he would approach regulatory issues with a presumption in favor of regulation by competitive market forces where possible. "Competition in a free market tends to maximize the public interest by providing a combination of goods and services reflecting consumer interests at competitive prices."[37]

Patrick said deregulation was not an end in itself, but it was a way of "maximizing the public interest."[38] He concluded his prepared remarks by shedding some insight into what he saw as appropriate first amendment freedoms. He said:

> The first amendment is the cornerstone of freedom in a democratic society. My commitment to competition in the economic marketplace parallels a strong commitment to free and open competition in the marketplace of ideas.[39]

Patrick refused to tip his hand as to where he stood on the broadcast fairness doctrine. In response to written questions by Senator Hollings which asked if he supported repeal of the fairness doctrine and equal time rule, Patrick merely said, "I think it is incumbent upon the congress and the Federal Communications Commission to constantly re-evaluate statutes and regulations, respectively, which affect the exercise of First Amendment rights by broadcast media."[40] Patrick said, "I have not yet had an opportunity to consider carefully and fully the effect of the Fairness Doctrine and the Equal Time rule on the exercise of First Amendment rights or the degree of competition in the political broadcasting market."[41] He avoided directly answering Hollings question by stating, "I am not prepared to reach any judgments prior to further, careful consideration. I do believe, however, that an open debate on the subject at this time would be worthwhile."[42]

As to whether Patrick agreed with the statement that repeal of any part of the fairness doctrine must be left to Congress, Patrick again replied evasively. He claimed that "regarding repeal of Section 315 of the Communications Act, the component parts of that section must be analyzed separately."[43] He believed that "Clearly, the equal opportunities provision of Section 315 is statutory, and therefore, can be repealed only by Congress."[44] However, "with respect to Section 315's reference to fairness doctrine obligations, there is a divergence of views as to whether the last sentence of Section 315, added in 1959 with the exceptions to equal opportunities, codified the fairness doctrine."[45] Patrick said he had not yet had an opportunity to carefully study this and, therefore, had "not yet reached a conclusion as to whether Congress codified the fairness doctrine."[46] Patrick concluded, in what would prove ironical, that it was his "hope and intention to cooperate fully with Congress in exchanging information.[47]

Broadcasting commented on the cordiality of Patrick's hearing. The only two members present were Goldwater, who chaired the hearing, and Senator Larry Pressler (R-South Dakota). As a result, according to *Broadcasting*, "Patrick's stand on many issues will remain unknown until he actually casts votes."[48] Broadcasters were concerned that with Patrick's Hollywood connections he would favor producers at their expense. Their fear was not to bear out.

Prior to his confirmation, Dennis Patrick had purposefully maintained a low profile. He refused to give his views on the record. But once seated he cautiously began to speak. In an April 9, 1984, *Broadcasting* interview, he said he hoped his words and deeds would mark him as a "responsible deregulator."[49] He said he would "approach every issue from the perspective of attempting to determine what is most consistent with the law and the public interest." He said the public interest "is not an absolute. It can change from issue to issue."[50]

On Wednesday, April 11, 1984, the FCC voted to begin a "comprehensive inquiry" into the legality and fairness of the fairness doctrine.[51] Fowler, Dawson and Quello voted for the inquiry. Rivera concurred and Patrick reserved his vote pending further study. Eventually, he voted with Fowler, Dawson and Quello. Fowler, in explaining the inquiry, claimed that special care had been taken to present the inquiry as "neutral." He said the inquiry would not start from the assumption that the doctrine can and should be repealed. Commissioner Dawson said it would be a "useful exercise." Commissioner Rivera, even though he criticized the action as a "frontal assault on the trustee concept of broadcasting," concurred with the commission decision to open the inquiry.[52]

The commission announced it would hold one or more *en banc* meetings "or some other oral procedures" at which the record of inquiry would be supplemented with opinions of legal scholars, communications experts, government policymakers and the public. Commenters would be asked to address 11 questions. Questions such as the necessity of the doctrine as a way to assure the public is exposed to diverse ideas, and whether the doctrine was constitutionally sound by imposing rules on broadcasters and not newspapers.[53]

Television Digest quoted Fowler as saying, "given recent court decisions limiting government regulations of speech, it may not be correct to apply the doctrine only to broadcasters in a rapidly expanding communications field."[54]   And commissioner Quello said the doctrine "just doesn't belong here any more."[55]

If the inquiry was to be "neutral," as Fowler said, general counsel Bruce Fein was anything but neutral. And Fein was responsible for preparing the inquiry. He said the inquiry included a section addressing the intent of Congress in imposing the fairness doctrine. Fein said a "search of laws couldn't find any evidence Congress limited FCC's discretion to modify doctrine."[56]

Congressional response was immediate. As *Broadcasting* reported it, "Two key congressional staffers last week stressed, underscored and warned that the FCC would be well advised not to attempt to repeal the fairness doctrine."[57]   The two staffers, Tom Rogers, majority counsel to the House Telecommunications Subcommittee, and Tom Cohen, minority counsel to the Senate Commerce Committee, both noted that Congress had kept the commission under close check. And, in a joint discussion at a telecommunications forum at George Washington University, they said that Congress would bring the same kind of pressure to bear in the event the commission attempted, in Cohen's words, to "mess around with it." In less than veiled terms, Rogers said "If commissioners take action ... they'll be in trouble."[58]

Fowler took his rallying cry directly to his broadcast public in an April 16, *Broadcasting* interview. Discusing the successes of his commission, he boldly claimed that "we have eliminated the terror factor in government."[59]

When asked whether the commission was ignoring the *Red Lion* decision in its current inquiry, Fowler replied:

> You're assuming the Red Lion decision and the facts underlying the Red Lion decision haven't changed. In fact, the factual basis underlying Red Lion has changed dramatically in both video and audio markets. I hope it's tested at some point. You're absolutely right that as a matter of law right now the court has said that the fairness doctrine is permissible under the First Amendment, although I frankly have trouble squaring that with the clear language in the First Amendment itself.[60]

And, when asked how he felt about the public interest standard, Fowler replied:

> The public interest standard is whatever the agency defines it to be. And I have said on many occasions that the public's interest defines the public interest. That's the way it's defined; through the

interreaction between the listener and the viewer and the broadcaster.[61]

And finally, in terms of his own neutrality on the issue of the fairness doctrine, he unequivocally stated:

The fairness doctrine has actually squelched the robust discussion of issues because broadcasters have been afraid that if they guess wrong in how they cover things, they're going to be subjected to fairness doctrine complaints, and called on the red carpet before the FCC, and possibly lose their license.[62]

The success of Fowler's ventures, as *Variety* reported, also rested on another variable, the results of the upcoming November elections.[63]

Seeking to build momentum for his newly opened fairness doctrine inquiry, Fowler tried to prod broadcasters to action in a Wednesday, May 2, 1984, speech at the closing session of the NAB convention. With his rallying cry, though, came a warning. His warning was "the end to constant government oversight won't work unless broadcasters take responsibility for ensuring that the public's interests and needs are met."[64] Commissioners Dawson and Patrick in separate appearances made the same pitch.[65]

In what appeared more an address to worried congressmen than optimistic broadcasters, Fowler said to those concerned that the FCC was taking deregulation too far, "Enforce we will and enforce we must."[66] Concluding, Fowler said the industry should show more concern for winning full first amendment rights.[67]

Tuesday, May 8, 1984, the FCC released its Notice of Inquiry on the fairness doctrine.[68] The Notice said the inquiry was to be a *preliminary* (emphasis added) analysis of the legal and policy underpinnings of the fairness doctrine. It suggested that "continuance of these obligations now or in the future may be at odds not only with the very same First Amendment goals underlying their foundation but with other First Amendment principles in other areas of speech and expression."[69] Comments were due August 6, and reply comments due by September 5, 1984.

Also in the second week of May, an attempt by Senator Bob Packwood to move his Freedom of Expression Act (S-1917) through his own Commerce Committee failed. Packwood had saved action on the bill for last on a busy 17 item agenda. But, he had to reschedule the mark-up for June 13 after the committee lost its quorum. Also, several Committee members had expressed serious reservations about the measure.[70]

President Reagan, Tuesday, May 15, 1984, announced his intention to renominate James Henry Quello to be a member of the FCC for a term of seven years from July 1, 1984.[71]

"Broadcasters are very pleased, " said Edward Fritts, president of the NAB of Quello's renomination. *Broadcasting* also said Quello's renomination was not hurt by his long-time association with House Energy and Commerce Committee chairman John Dingell (D-Michigan). "We remain good friends on a personal basis, even though professionally there are certain areas on which we don't agree," Quello said.[72] The disagreements on professional matters was obviously an understatement.

In the last week of August, as if in reply to Fowler's convention urging, the NAB Executive Committee authorized three studies designed to show the "chilling effect" of the fairness doctrine, and to dispute scarcity argument for its retention.[73] Two of the studies were to be in-house NAB studies. One would analyze 100-150 markets at various stages of development in a variety of broadcast areas. The second in-house study would be a market-by-market survey of stations looking for instances where broadcasters had been less than robust in news coverage because of alleged fear of repercussions caused by the fairness doctrine.[74] The third study was targeted at showing that economics, not scarcity, was a controlling factor. The study would survey startup and operational costs for 3 years of newspapers, TV and radio stations.[75]

The nomination hearing for James Quello's renomination was held Thursday, June 7, 1984.[76] In his opening statement, Quello spelled out his philosophy:

> My philosophy is that I think we should regulate in a spirit of mutual cooperation with the regulated businesses, rather than assume right from the start an adversary role. I think we should reserve the adversary role for egregious cases.[77]

When asked by Senator Goldwater to give his position on legislation to do away with both Section 315 and the fairness doctrine, Quello replied:

> I have a longstanding record of advocating the abolition of section 315 and the Fairness Doctrine.
>
> ...

However, in the recent FCC inquiry, I did mention that the Fairness Doctrine encompassed in a statute, and hence, is more a prerogative of Congress than the FCC. The Commission should have a very neutral inquiry to find out from legal and legislative experts what they think about the Fairness Doctrine as it applies to communications today.

...

There is a question [in the inquiry] on whether the Fairness Doctrine is mandated or not. My presumption is that it is, and there would be a burden of proof that it is not.[78]

The question of the doctrine's statutory basis was now quite salient. Particularly in view of the commission's fairness doctrine Inquiry. Senator Hollings, for instance, submitted numerous questions on issues surrounding the fairness doctrine. Hollings asked Quello if he had ever voted in favor of a commission order stating that the fairness doctrine was a statutory requirement? Quello replied that he had many times supported orders "which either stated, or strongly implied, that Fairness Doctrine has a statutory basis."[79]

When Hollings asked Quello if he had ever stated in a speech, article, testimony before Congress, or elsewhere that the fairness doctrine was a statutory requirement or that legislation was required for its repeal, Quello replied:

I have often publicly stated my view that the Fairness Doctrine was codified by the 1959 amendment to the Communications Act. On April 11th of this year, I issued a statement accompanying a Notice of Inquiry on the Fairness Doctrine in which I said: "the Commission has long acquiesced in the view that the 1959 amendments to the Communications Act did effect a codification of the doctrine, and I believe that the burden of proof rests on those who seek to change this status quo."[80]

In his prepared statement though, Quello was not as firm in his resolution of the doctrine's statutory basis. Speaking of the commission's Notice of Inquiry, he said:

It is no secret that I have long advocated full First Amendment rights for the electronic media. I strongly endorse the thrust of this document which has many well-reasoned arguments and which should provoke thoughtful comments.[81]

He continued:

> I would like to add that I shall be very interested in reviewing the comments concerning the Commission's statutory authority to revise the fairness doctrine. The Commission has long acquiesced in the view that the 1959 amendments to the Communications Act did effect a codification of the doctrine, and I believe that the burden of proof rests on those who seek to change this status quo. I trust that this issue will be addressed at length in the comments, and I look forward to examining the views of legal scholars on this issue.

Notwithstanding the above discussion, *Broadcasting* characterized Quello's confirmation hearing as non-controversial, saying it was as easy "as ice cream on a hot summer day."[82]

On June 11, 1984, *Broadcasting* ran a profile of Bruce Fein. As described by *Broadcasting*, "Bruce Elliot Fein, the FCC's 37-year-old general counsel . . . isn't afraid to say what's on his mind, even when it raises the hackles of the FCC's congressional overseers or grates upon the sensibilities of commission colleagues."[83] He had written many legal articles, including one he wrote for the legal magazine *District Lawyer*, titled "Fighting Off Congress--A Bill of Rights for Independent Agencies." This article caused House Telecommunications Subcommittee Chairman Timothy Wirth (D-Colorado) to chastise Fein at an February 8, 1984, oversight hearing.[84]

The strain Fowler's general counsel caused with Congress did not seem to bother Fowler. *Broadcasting* quoted Fowler as saying of Fein, "What Bruce stands for, and indeed has dedicated his life to, is promoting and advancing the cause of individual freedom."[85] Broadcasters certainly believed he had advanced their individual freedoms.

In an interview for the *Broadcasting* profile, Fein expressed distaste for the fairness doctrine. He said he believed the FCC could, without congressional approval, "revoke the fairness doctrine as it applies to all aspects of broadcasting, except insofar as broadcasters covering political campaigns."[86] He was pleased that the commission had "achieved success in at least raising the level of discourse regarding the fairness doctrine."[87]

According to Mass Media Bureau chief James McKinney, there would now be "no standards," as a result of the commission's June 27 action deregulating television that virtually duplicated radio deregulation.[88] The FCC in this Report and Order deleted rules and guidelines applied to television, including programming content; program logging; ascertainment of community needs; and limits on number and length of commercials. McKinney in announcing the commission's action said, "stations are [now] free to decide what to cover and how."[89] The commission's vote was unanimous, except for commissioner Rivera's concurring in general on deregulation, but dissenting to all parts dealing with children's television programming.[90]

The decision to deregulate television pleased both commercial and noncommercial broadcasters. But Congress and interest groups were less enthused.[91] House Telecommunications Subcommittee Chairman Timothy Wirth (D-Colorado) said the commission's actions were "totally unjustified."[92] Andrew Schwartzman, executive director of the Media Access Project, called the FCC's action a "cynical fraud on the American public."[93] He identified the real peril of the commission decision by saying, "It [is] distressing to see the FCC say it will be placing an increased reliance on citizen complaints for enforcement while removing meaningful program logs as a mechanism for citizens to review broadcasting performance."[94] And Cathy Boggs, policy analyst for the Telecommunications Research and Action Center, said "We think the James Watt of the airwaves has struck again."[95] TRAC announced it planned to appeal the commission decision.

Television deregulation was a victory for Mark Fowler. He said the decision "removes an unnecessary layers of government involvement in the television program decisions of the American people. There is no need for rigid guidelines on commercial time limits and formalistic ascertainment procedures."[96] As quoted by *Variety*, Fowler said he still had two more rules "targeted for the scrap heap."[97] These were the 7-7-7 group ownership rules and the fairness doctrine.

The Supreme Court, the first week of July, declared unconstitutional a ban against editorials on TV-radio stations that receive federal funds. The case, *FCC v. League of Women Voters*,[98] stemmed from a 1979 challenge by L.A.-based Pacifica Foundation, licensee of five public radio stations. Pacifica was joined in its challenge by Representative Waxman (D-California) and the League of Women Voters. Together, they challenged an FCC ban on public station editorials. The Carter Administration decided in 1979 not to contest the issue, but the Reagan Administration did.   The U.S. District Court, central California, ruled initially against the Reagan Administration.   But, on appeal the Supreme Court threw out the public station editorial ban.   It said stations may air editorials provided they run a disclaimer that the editorial is not necessarily the federal government's view.   In the majority were Justices Brennan, Marshall, Powell, O'Connor and Blackmun.

The U.S. Supreme Court majority opinion written by Justice Brennan also included two footnotes that gave new ammunition to those supporting a move to abolish the fairness doctrine.   Opponents of the doctrine called the decision a clear signal that the Court was ready to reconsider *Red Lion*.[99]   The language in Footnote 11 dealt with the concept of spectrum scarcity, and stated:

> The prevailing rational for broadcast regulation based on spectrum scarcity has come under increasing criticism in recent years.   Critics, including the chairman of the FCC, charge that with the advent of cable and satellite television technology, communities now have access to such a wide variety of stations that the scarcity doctrine is obsolete...   We are not prepared, however, to reconsider our long-standing approach without some signal from Congress or the FCC that technological developments have advanced so far that some revision of the system of broadcast regulation may be required.[100]

The language in Footnote 12 dealt with the concept of "chilling speech" and said:

> We note that the FCC, observing that 'if any substantial possibility exists that the [fairness doctrine] rules have impeded, rather than furthered, First Amendment objectives, repeal may be warranted on that ground alone,' has tentatively concluded that the rules, by effectively chilling speech, do not serve the public interest and has therefore proposed to repeal them...   Of course, the Commission may, in the exercise of its discretion, decide to modify or abandon these rules, and we express no view on the legality of either course. As we recognized in *Red Lion*, however, were it to be shown by the Commission that the fairness doctrine 'has the effect of reducing rather than enhancing' speech, we would then be forced to reconsider the constitutional basis of our decision in that case.[101]

Fowler said he was "extremely heartened" by the decision. "For the first time, the Supreme Court has recognized that the scarcity argument may not be sound."[102] Fowler also welcomed that the court may be prepared to reconsider its ruling in *Red Lion* regarding the constitutionality of the fairness doctrine if a "chilling effect" could be shown.[103]

Not surprisingly, in an interview with *Television Digest*, FCC general counsel Bruce Fein said Footnote 11 was "enormously significant" in the fight against the fairness doctrine, "because it puts broadcasters in a position to receive the same First Amendment rights as the print media."[104] Fein claimed the reference to *Red Lion* also was significant because "new players on the Court" indicated "a favorable inclination" to revisit "the chilling effect" of the doctrine. "Otherwise why would the Court repeat what it has already said."[105]

NAB general counsel, and former Mass Media bureau deputy chief, Henry Bauman predicted the FCC would "seize the opportunity to get something moving as soon as possible."[106] The broadcast industry's trade press was a buzz with speculation of what case would be used to test how far the Supreme Court was willing to go in rethinking scarcity rationale and validity of the doctrine.[107]

Not everyone saw the footnotes as that compelling. Commissioner Rivera said "everybody [favoring repeal of the doctrine] is reading too much into those footnotes." He said the Court was just being "prudent" in repeating what it already had said in *Red Lion*, and that "if things change, we want to know about it."

Senator Bob Packwood said "If I've ever seen an invitation to bring a case, there it is."[108] Packwood said the footnotes were sending a strong signal to the FCC or Congress or broadcasters "to bring us a case and lay the ground work for the argument that the scarcity argument is no longer valid."[109] He said he planned talking with the NAB and others in the broadcasting industry about choosing the "right case" to bring before the court.[110] Timothy Dyk, who prepared an *amicus* brief on behalf of CBS, the NAB and the Radio-Television News Directors Association, noted that whether or not the court intended the invitation, "it's an invitation."[111]

Fowler's deregulatory vision was buoyed by the decision. This optimism was evident in a July 23, 1984, interview with *U.S. News & World Report*. When asked if the FCC, as an agency, really was not necessary, Fowler replied:

We only need it to resolve problems of interference, to insure that stations operate on the correct power on the correct frequency.[112]

He also reiterated his faith in allowing markets to work:

I believe in promoting individualism in a free society as opposed to relying on the heavy hand of government. I don't believe, generally, that bureaucrats need to guide people's decision or control their lives, and I approach every issue with a presumption against government intervention unless there is a compelling need.[113]

With comments on its fairness doctrine Inquiry due by August 6, and encouraged by the recent Supreme Court case, the FCC made a final push to get the support and action of broadcasters. This was typified in FCC Mass Media bureau chief James McKinney's Friday, August 17th speech to the West Virginia Association of Broadcasters. He criticized the broadcast industry for not fighting harder for repeal of fairness doctrine. "You seem unwilling to stand up and be counted when we ask for examples of the 'chilling effect' our remaining programming policies have on your journalistic freedoms," McKinney said.[114]

"Don't remain silent," McKinney said, especially now that the U.S. Supreme Court had issued an "open invitation... to revisit the whole issue." He continued that he would challenge broadcasters "to consider why it is that the Commission is leading the local broadcasters on this issue. ... this is not the time to take it easy. The Commission has fired the starting gun but the industry must run the race."[115]

McKinney said of the fairness doctrine, "If its continued implementation imposes self-censorship on the broadcasters resulting in the actual avoidance of controversial issues in order to prevent triggering other, 'balanced' or 'fair' programing, the deed of censorship is done. And censorship, whether imposed directly by government or indirectly by a doctrine created by the government is equally dangerous."[116]

An interesting side note into the functioning of the current commission was provided by McKinney in an August 27, *Broadcasting*, interview. There he said that "If FCC policies and rules aren't any good, get rid of them; but if they're on the books, enforce them."[117] But then he went on to say he had "difficulty sometimes" getting a majority of the commissioners to go along with him when he felt enforcement was warranted.[118]   He concluded with this telling statement, "This is not a strong enforcement commission."[119]

Reply comments on the FCC's fairness doctrine inquiry were due by September 5, and only ABC among broadcast groups failed to call for the doctrine's outright repeal.[120]   Those favoring repeal of doctrine argued that it was unconstitutional; inhibiting; chilling; no longer needed under scarcity factor; it failed to achieve its goals; and the FCC had ample authority to act without congressional guidance.[121]

Whether the commission could eliminate the doctrine without congressional approval proved controversial.   Tim Dyk, writing for CBS declared: "A decision by the Commission that it has authority to rescind the doctrine would be entitled to substantial judicial deference. This flows from the 'venerable principle that the construction of a statute by those charged with its execution should be followed unless there are compelling indications that it is wrong' (*Red Lion Broadcasting vs. FCC*)... The most reasonable interpretation of Section 315(a) is that it allows, but does not require, enforcement of the fairness doctrine... It is clearly within the Commission's discretion to rescind the doctrine."[122]   The RTNDA, the Evening News Association, Gannett Co., and Gaylord Broadcasting agreed with CBS's reasoning.

The National Telecommunications and Information Administration (NTIA), however, said its review uncovered "compelling evidence" that Congress had, in fact, incorporated the doctrine into the 1959 amendment.[123]   "This leads us to conclude that it is congress, and not the commission, which is the appropriate forum to resolve the future of the fairness doctrine."[124]   Understandably, interest groups such as MAP, TRAC and DNC, also argued that the commission could not act without legislation.

MAP and TRAC said that most "distressing" was the fact that the FCC even launched inquiry.   "Instead of collecting information and making recommendations to Congress, the Commission has... undertaken to redefine and expand its own authority far beyond Congress' delegation... It has recast itself as legislator and judge... deciding whether its own [enabling] statute is constitutional."[125]

Fowler in an attempt to improve congressional relations, the last week of September announced two key staff changes. First, legislative affairs efforts, then with the General Counsel Office, would be shifted to Office of Public Affairs under Chief William Russell. Second, the chairman would add a professional to his personal staff to work primarily on Congressional relations.[126] These recommendations were approved on December 10. It was reported that these actions came at the suggestion of the new, less contentious, FCC general counsel designate Jack Smith. Smith would assume duties of the general counsel officially in October.

Smith saw the role of the general counsel differently from his predecessor, Bruce Fein. Reportedly, one of Smith's first activities was meeting with James McKinney and convincing him to take jurisdiction over the Notice of Inquiry on the fairness doctrine. That initiative had been begun by Fein, but Smith said he believed the general counsel should not initiate policy.

The FCC decided Friday, October 26, 1984, that WTVH(TV) Syracuse violated the fairness doctrine. WTVH had violated the doctrine by airing 182 minutes of spot ads advocating construction of a nearby nuclear power plant as a "sound investment" without adequately presenting contrasting viewpoints.[127]

This was the first time in five years that the commission had found a TV licensee in violation of the fairness doctrine. Some thought it came suspiciously amid the controversial commission inquiry into whether the doctrine was required under the Communication Act. The vote was 4-1. Fowler voted with a majority of commissioners Rivera, Patrick and Quello (who concurred), while commissioner Dawson dissented.[128]

At issue in the decision was a series of editorial advertisements television station WTVH Syracuse ran for the Energy Association of New York, a trade association for utilities, from July 7 to September 7, 1982. The ads advocated the continued construction of the Nine Mile II nuclear plant in upstate New York. The Syracuse Peace Council alleged the ads presented only one side of the nuclear plant's being a "sound investment" in New York's future. Syracuse had asked the station to "correct the programing imbalance." The station did not, and the group brought its complaint to the FCC in November 1983. WTVH contended that the ads were really about eliminating the dependency on foreign oil and the need for electricity, and no controversial issues of public importance were at issue.[129] WTVH had run 182 minutes of ads for the utility lobby during the period, but had only provided 22 minutes of coverage to contrasting views.[130]

Henry Rivera may have captured the situation best. He said that in past fairness doctrine cases the FCC repeatedly had told complainants they failed to make a case for one reason or another. Explaining the present case, he drew a parallel to a shell game. Rivera said "we keep moving the pea around" on complainants, "and this time they found the pea."[131]

The *Syracuse* case provided new FCC general counsel Jack Smith with a case to argue if the commission's findings were appealed. And few questioned the case would not be appealed. At a press conference on October 26, Smith said his office had given the Mass Media Bureau responsibly for handling the commission's notice of inquiry on the fairness doctrine.[132] Now with a case the General Counsel's Office no longer needed to be involved directly in setting policy. It had the opportunity to test the policy in court.

A November 5, 1984, *Broadcasting* editorial showed what the commission's only negative fairness doctrine decision in six years could do to rally broadcasters. In one stroke, it accomplished what four years of prodding by the commission itself could not accomplish. The editorial began with the statement that "The FCC has proved once again that it is the prisoner of its fairness doctrine."[133] Interestingly, one would think the editors would cast the issue in first amendment terms, but it actually cast the issue more in economic terms:

> [B]roadcasters are reminded of the perils of accepting advertising that may trigger fairness complaints. The bottom-line question is: How many spots must be sold to offset the possible legal fees? At the Wharton school they'd say that's no way to run a business.[134]

On December 10, 1984, the commission approved the consolidation of the Office of Public Affairs, the legislative affairs functions of the Office of General Counsel and the congressional correspondence function of the Office of the Chairman into the Office of Congressional and Public Affairs. The reorganization had a stated function of creating an organizational structure for "communicating the commission's policies regarding telecommunications to the Congress, the news media and the public," by combining these similar activities into a single bureau level entity.[135]

Also approved was a new position, Special Assistant to the Chairman for Congressional Affairs. The position was filled by Raymond L. Strassburger, who worked on communications issues as an aide to the Senate Commerce, Science and Transportation Committee, as an FCC staffer and, most recently, as assistant director of Times Mirror Co.'s Washington office.[136]   Strassburger's assignment was to keep in close touch with House and Senate Commerce Committee staffers.

A December 10, 1984, *Broadcasting* profile of Dennis Patrick claimed he hoped for reappointment when his term expired June 30, 1985.[137] The initial concerns broadcasters had of Patrick seemed to have eased. Jeff Baumann, former Mass Media bureau deputy chief and now senior vice president and general counsel for the NAB, said of Patrick, that "while broadcasters don't always agree that the marketplace is an appropriate answer to all regulatory issues, we have always found him open to our point of view."[138]

Broadcasting pointed out that if Patrick was reappointed, his importance to broadcasters would surely grow. As one of only two Republicans remaining at the FCC if Fowler resigned, Patrick could very well be the next FCC chairman.[139] As for as Fowler's and his relationship, Patrick said "Mark and I are friends, and I make no bones about that."[140]

1985

As mentioned above, the commission's ruling in the Meredith case was especially notable. It was the only violation the commission found in the 20 fairness doctrine cases it handled in 1984. Staff attorneys were said to have resolved another 1,000 fairness complaints. But more importantly, the Meredith ruling was the only fairness doctrine violation the commission had found since 1979. It may have been the found "pea" that Rivera claimed. It could also have been a planted "pea." It was not an especially egregious case. And WTVH had actually rectified the imbalance before the commission's finding. It was no surprise then when Meredith appealed the commission finding in April.

1985 would prove a significant year for the future of the fairness doctrine. Open hearings were held by the commission in January to hear evidence for its fairness inquiry. The commission went out of its way to encourage industry participation in these hearings.

The anecdotal instances broadcasters provided were given special focus and attention when the commission released its findings in August. The Fairness Report released in August provided a construction of what the commission had supported since Fowler came on in 1981. It denied scarcity was any longer a factor, and it found the doctrine "chilled" speech. The commission also concluded the doctrine was "probably" codified, but based on the record collected, its constitutionality was now suspect. The Report was an invitation to challenge the doctrine. RTNDA and other media organizations did just that in October. The Report also strained congressional/commission relations even further.

A number of developments relating to the fairness doctrine occurred during the second week of January 1985. First, on Wednesday, January 9, WTVH(TV) Syracuse's owner, Meredith Broadcasting, notified the commission it would petition for reconsideration of its decision within thirty days.[141] And, at its only January meeting on Thursday, January 10th, the commission dismissed a Central Intelligence Agency complaint that ABC had violated the fairness doctrine and personal attack rules.[142] The CIA had claimed ABC presented intentional news distortion by alleging that the CIA plotted to kill a Honolulu businessman.[143]

Also, at its January meeting the commission announced it would hold open hearings on Thursday and Friday, February 7 and 8, as part of its general Inquiry into the fairness doctrine. Commissioners took special pains to make sure industry interests participated.

There were two additional fairness doctrine developments during the second week of January. First, for the fifth time in five Congresses, Senator Proxmire (D-Wisconsin) introduced a bill to eliminate the equal time rule and the fairness doctrine.[144] Proxmire's bill, S-22, also would have repealed program objectivity standards and the political editorializing ban for public broadcasters. It also "clarified the term 'public interest, convenience, and (sic) necessity'."[145] The final fairness doctrine development this week was a Supreme Court denial, without comment, to review the commission's and a lower court ruling sought by American Security Council. ASC claimed CBS had violated the fairness doctrine in 1981 documentary on Defense Department titled "Defense of America." The commission had denied ASC's petition, and the lower court had upheld the commission's decision.[146]

On Wednesday, February 6, the day before the FCC's *en banc* hearings were scheduled to start, Representative Dingell, serving as spokesman of a coalition formed to lobby to retain the fairness doctrine, held a press conference. There, the coalition announced their opposition to the proceedings. The coalition was called Campaign for Free Speech, and was composed of 17 labor, public interest and religious organizations.[147] At the news conference, Dingell argued that the doctrine had been effective in protecting the public interest for 50 years, and that it was "absolutely fundamental to the protection of our First Amendment free speech rights."[148]

Advocates for and against repeal of the doctrine, some 37 in all, had been invited by the commission to discuss their views in six panels.[149] And at the start of the hearing on February 7, the members of the coalition Campaign for Free Speech also issued a statement saying their participation should not "be construed as endorsing either the FCC's decision to conduct this inquiry at all or the manner in which it has been administered."[150]

But the broadcasters and media organizations had their big guns there to argue in opposition to the doctrine. And their testimony is what received wide coverage. Attorney Timothy Dyk, representing CBS, claimed the doctrine was not a statutory requirement (an argument he had also made in 1969 in a filing in the *Red Lion* case). Dyk gave a history of the doctrine. His history concluded that the commission did have the authority to delete the fairness requirement from its regulations.[151] Dyk said there was "no support" for the argument that Congress compelled the FCC to adopt the fairness doctrine. He also said he did not think the courts would overrule the commission, should it decide to eliminate the obligation. He continued that even if the commission decided the statute bars it from eliminating the doctrine, the FCC should address the basis for the doctrine's continued constitutionality. "The Supreme Court relies very heavily on this agency," Dyk said.[152]

NAB senior vice president and general counsel, Henry Baumann, was less confident of the commission's ability to dismiss the fairness doctrine on its own. But, he said the fairness doctrine was "in plain violation of the First Amendment [and] is unacceptable not only because it controls content ... but [also] because the fairness doctrine accomplishes what it set out to avoid."[153]

Bruce Fein, former FCC general counsel and currently with the Washington public relations firm of Gray & Co., spoke of the doctrine's lack of constitutional grounding. Fein said that unless the FCC could "affirmatively explain" why the fairness doctrine was necessary, the obligation should be "forthrightly" discarded.[154]

Former FCC chairman Charles Ferris, who favored retaining the doctrine, disputed the claim that broadcasters would likely air more controversial programming without the doctrine than with it. Ferris argued that most broadcasters would not air controversial viewpoints anyway, because their advertisers "don't want to be associated with the unpopular, with that which is out of vogue."[155]

After the two days of hearings Fowler said the "next step" would be to analyze the record and discuss the matter further with Congress.[156] As neutrally as Fowler presented this conclusion, a more realistic view of the intent, and tone, of these hearings can be seen in how *Variety* discussed the hearings. *Variety* said "The FCC began two days of public hearings last week on the Fairness Doctrine, an exercise its chairman hopes will one day result in termination of the policy."[157]

Broadcasting, February 18, ran a feature on Mark Fowler's chairmanship. Commissioners, and others, gave their perceptions of Fowler's successes. Commissioner Mimi Dawson attributed Fowler's success to his managerial abilities. She said, "He had a clear goal; he had a clear philosophy, and he knew how and why he was doing it. That put us on a faster track, and a more stable track, than most commissions." She continued, saying that she tells "broadcasters that they're very lucky to have had someone who knows the area so well that he could come in and hit the ground running and move rapidly."[158]

Commissioner Dennis Patrick said one of Fowler's major accomplishments lay in "changing the terms of the debate." Patrick said Fowler had changed the agency's threshold question. Patrick said, now the question had become whether the FCC should regulate at all, not what sort of regulation might be appropriate.[159] Commissioner Quello spoke in a similar vein. He said that Fowler's initiation of the fairness inquiry questioning whether the FCC could repeal the fairness doctrine "at least raised the question."[160]

Not everyone, though, had as much respect for Fowler. TRAC's Simon, for instance, said what Fowler's early open-door policy turned out to mean in practice was that Fowler "was always willing to repeat his point of view."[161]

Broadcasting also put into perspective some of the difficulties Fowler had encountered, especially in Congress. It claimed Fowler's uncompromising spirit was responsible, at least in part, for the agency's rocky relationship with Congress. His early recommendation to Congress to repeal the fairness doctrine and equal opportunities law obligations, and his advocacy of Stephen Sharp, the chairman's general counsel, for a commission seat over the candidate of the Republican-controlled Senate Commerce Committee, all worked against congenial relations.[162]

The same February 18 issue of *Broadcasting* also featured an interview with Fowler, titled "Quotations from the Chairman." When *Broadcasting* asked if in his mind the fairness doctrine was codified, Fowler replied:

> I will reserve my judgment until we look at the record. I think there are some very good arguments that it is codified, but there are other arguments that suggest it is not. I haven't had a chance to parse through all that to make a final determination in my own mind.[163]

And when asked if there was any single big item left on his agenda, Fowler said:

> Yes. I sound like I'm fixated on this, but I'm still dedicated to the effort to remove content regulation. Although we have come a long way, there is still a long way to go, and everybody recognizes that.[164]

Finally in February, in an address before the National Telephone Cooperative[165] on Tuesday, February 26, Fowler identified his political philosophy as that of "conservative populism." He explained this as being a philosophy:

> [B]ased on the need to free the initiative of today's common man from the vested interest of a vast, bureaucratic government. I believe that Americans of the information age are making their frontiers ones of the mind and its inventions, and ones of the spirit. We must not let pervasive government intervention bring the wagon train of human technological achievement and personal service to a belabored halt.

He concluded this speech by saying that during his chairmanship he had tried to "turn this political philosophy into a regulatory policy."

The White House, on Thursday, March 7, interviewed Dennis Patrick for reappointment to 7-year term. The Administration was interviewing no other candidates, and it was expected Patrick would get the White House approval.[166]

The Senate Subcommittee on Communications held an FCC authorization and oversight hearing[167] on Wednesday, March 20. An indication of its tone can be gleaned from the opening statement of Senator Hollings:

> I have often said that there is no education in the second kick of a mule. During the last Congress, the Chairman of the FCC proved that old adage correct. He, however, appears to be showing that three kicks might do the trick.[168]

Saying that in the past two years, Congress had become very adept at overturning decisions of the commission, Hollings claimed that, with certain exceptions, most commission decisions mistakenly had been "based more on faith than fact."[169]

Hollings warned Fowler that he was "particularly concerned about the various proceedings concerning the fairness doctrine. But in a subtle shift of focus, Hollings seemed particularly interested in protecting personal attack and political editorializing rules." He warned Fowler:

> Since the beginning of Chairman Fowler's tenure, I have put him on notice not to weaken in any way the various political broadcasting laws or rules. So that there is no misunderstanding, the Chairman should consider such notice to be again issued.[170]

In written responses to questions submitted to the commission prior to the hearings by Senators Packwood and Goldwater, Fowler said of the agency's current fairness doctrine inquiry:

> [T]he Notice questions whether retention of the doctrine was necessary or appropriate in light of present marketplace conditions. The Notice also explored the Commission's authority to substantially modify or repeal the Fairness Doctrine absent specific statutory authorization in light of the requirements of section 315 and the general public interest standard of the Communications Act of 1934, as amended.

The Notice of Inquiry also examined the question of whether the Fairness Doctrine is constitutionally mandated or even constitutionally permissible. Recognizing that as a content-based regulation, the Fairness Doctrine is an exception to the First Amendment's guarantees, the Notice inquired as to whether the doctrine is necessary to further the governmental interest in an informed electorate and suggested that in operation, it may have an impermissible "chilling" effect on the free expression of ideas. We expect that the Commission's conclusions in this area may be of particular use to the courts on this question.[171]

Addressing an ABA seminar in Washington on Friday, March 29, Dennis Patrick claimed the U.S. Supreme Court had shown it was "getting itchy" on the fairness doctrine. He said he believed that if presented with persuasive evidence it might rule the doctrine unconstitutional. He was referring to the 1984 *League of Women Voters*[172] case which struck down the ban on political editorializing on public TV. Patrick said the justices "implied that unless a content restriction is the least restrictive alternative," it's unconstitutional.[173]

During the first week of April, the ABA sponsored a conference on communications law in Washington. Dennis Patrick, speaking there, said he had "tentatively concluded" that Congress had codified the doctrine when it amended Section 315 of the Communications Act in 1959. "So I do not believe the FCC should repeal the doctrine," Patrick said.[174]

At the same forum, Daniel Brenner, senior adviser to Fowler, and the man behind the idea of Fowler's original spectrum fee proposal, said he still believed that a spectrum fee should be assessed. "That's the quid pro quo," he said. Brenner said there should be a "well-funded" public broadcasting system to "meet the needs that we feel should be met," but may not be in a deregulated commercial broadcasting environment.[175] Dan Brenner had served in a close policy position in both the Fowler and Ferris commissions. Ferris hired Brenner as one of his assistants in 1979, and Brenner remained when Fowler replaced Ferris in 1981. He eventually came to serve as Fowler's unofficial speech writer and close advisor.[176]

In the second week of April, Meredith Corp., notified the FCC it would pursue "all legal remedies" to reverse the commission decision finding WTVH(TV) Syracuse in violation of the fairness doctrine. Meredith, in its filing, said "It's time for a court review of the fairness doctrine to reject the government's clumsy effort to program TV stations.[177]

At a NAB convention panel, the third week of April, James Quello and Mimi Dawson both indicated that the commission would defer to Congress on the fairness doctrine issue. Also on the panel, Mass Media Bureau chief McKinney indicated the commission expected to act by late June on its fairness doctrine Inquiry. During his presentation Quello gave a clue that maybe the commission's Meredith vote was more than dutiful enforcement. As he said, "With our vote we may have given Meredith a chance. . . to have the Supreme Court rule on the constitutionality issue."[178]

By the end of April, both Mark Fowler and Bert Halprin, chief of its Common Carrier bureau, were denying rumors that they may be leaving. But commissioner Henry Rivera, a Democrat, had made no secret of his job negotiations with outside law firms.[179] Rivera was one of the few dissenters in a number of FCC decisions. April 21, 1985, the *Washington Post* reported that Rivera, without setting a date, said he was leaving the commission for personal reasons.[180]

On Wednesday, May 1, 1985, Senator Packwood (R-Oregon) reintroduced his Freedom of Expression Act to repeal the fairness doctrine and equal time rules. The bill was identical to his S-1917 from the last Congress. It was cosponsored by Senator Goldwater, chairman of the Senate Communications Subcommittee.[181] Although Senator Packwood was now Finance Committee chairman, he had promised to continue the campaign he began as chairman of the Commerce Committee to remove content rules for television and radio.

President Reagan announced on Thursday, May 30, his intention to renominate Dennis R. Patrick as an FCC commissioner. Patrick, who had been a commissioner since 1983, was to be reappointed for a term of 7 years from July 1, 1985.[182]

FCC commissioner Dennis Patrick's confirmation hearing before the Senate Commerce Committee,[183] Thursday, July 11, was chaired by Senate Communications Subcommittee chairman Barry Goldwater. *Broadcasting* described the hearing as, "a cordial, 20-minute session."[184] Patrick's nomination was approved at a committee markup on Thursday, July 18.

At the hearing there were no questions from the floor directed to Patrick about the fairness doctrine. Senator Hollings had submitted questions to Patrick prior to his hearing, though, and one did address

Patrick's stand on the issue. Hollings had asked Patrick his views of the fairness doctrine, including the FCC's recent record of administration and enforcement. Patrick said he thought "that congress probably codified the Fairness Doctrine when it amended Section 315 of the Act in 1959. Therefore, it is my tentative conclusion that the Commission lacks the authority to repeal it."[185] He continued though, saying:

> As a policy matter, however, I have reservations as to whether the Fairness Doctrine serves the public interest. ... My reasons are two-fold. First, the notion of "scarcity," upon which the Supreme Court relied in *Red Lion* when it upheld the doctrine's limitations on the First Amendment, is suspect in today's marketplace. Second, I am concerned about the doctrine's chilling effect on broadcasters, something about which we received a good deal of testimony at our *en banc* hearings earlier this year. If the effective result of the doctrine is that viewers are receiving less information because of chilling, then the doctrine may not be serving the public interest.[186]

In answer to the second part of Hollings' question, on the FCC's record of enforcement, Patrick said:

> As long as the Fairness Doctrine remains the law, it is incumbent upon the FCC to enforce it faithfully. Administration of the doctrine is difficult, requiring very subjective decisions to be made upon which reasonable people may differ. Nonetheless, to my knowledge the Commission has made a good faith effort to administer and enforce the doctrine. I voted to find a fairness doctrine violation this year (in the *Syracuse Peace Council* case) and I will again if other violations occur.[187]

An August 5, *Business Week*, article asserted that Fowler was shopping for a fairness doctrine test case to bring before the U.S. Supreme Court.[188] *Business Week* pointed out that in his arguments against government interference in broadcasting, Fowler "is given to drawing dire analogies with Nazi Germany."[189] It also said that "the most recent rumors give Dennis R. Patrick the inside track" as Fowler's successor. It cited "one insider" who predicted that, as chairman, Patrick would "out-Fowler Fowler."[190]

The FCC, August 7, concluded its Inquiry into the fairness doctrine.[191] Voting 4-0, the FCC concluded the fairness doctrine was not in the public interest and, contrary to its intended purposes, inhibited broadcasters from presenting controversial issues of public importance. The FCC, however, said it would continue to enforce the doctrine, even though such enforcement infringes on "fundamental constitutional principles," furnishes the government with a "dangerous" tool that could be abused, and imposes unnecessary costs on broadcasters and the FCC.[192]

Much of the FCC's 111-page report was devoted to providing a record of the doctrine's "chilling effect," and the increase in the number and type of information sources available.[193]   What the commission had done was develop a "voluminous record compiled during the inquiry"[194] supporting its own view, that the doctrine resulted in the opposite of its intended effect.

Part of the intent of the inquiry was to show that *Red Lion* relied on a previous commission's assertion that the fairness doctrine did not operate to inhibit the coverage of controversial issues of public importance.   Not surprisingly, the commission concluded "The evidence in this proceeding, however, compels the conclusion that this assumption is no longer valid."[195]   It also noted that *Red Lion* had been premised on the marketplace that existed 16 years ago, and it concluded, "In recent years, there has been a significant increase in the number and types of information sources."[196]

The FCC did not definitively decide, though, whether the doctrine was codified by 1959 amendments to the Communications Act. The commission said, it was "not necessary" for the commission "to definitively resolve whether or not it has the requisite statutory authority to eliminate the doctrine."[197]   The Report said the commission would "afford Congress the opportunity to review the doctrine in light of the record produced by the inquiry, whose record will be forwarded to Congress."[198]

Prior to this Inquiry, the commission had to rely on the finding of the 1974 Fairness Report.   There, the commission had upheld the doctrine's validity. It now had a new official finding to draw on. One that supported its current view. This was particularly true of their finding on the doctrine's constitutionality:

> We believe that there are serious questions raised with respect to the constitutionality of the fairness doctrine whether or not the Supreme Court chooses to continue to apply the less exacting standard which it has traditionally employed in assessing the constitutionality of broadcast regulation.

The compelling evidence in this proceeding demonstrates that the fairness doctrine, in operation, inhibits the presentation of controversial issues of public importance. As a consequence, even under a standard of review short of the strict scrutiny standard applied to test the constitutionality of restraints on the press, we believe that the fairness doctrine can no longer be justified on the ground that it is necessary to promote the First Amendment rights of the viewing and listening public. Indeed, the chilling effect on the presentation of controversial issues of public importance resulting from our regulatory policies affirmatively disserves the interest of the public in obtaining access to diverse viewpoints. In addition, we believe that the fairness doctrine, as a regulation which directly affects the content of speech aired over broadcast frequencies, significantly impairs the journalistic freedom of broadcasters.[199]

Most believed that the FCC would not likely challenge the constitutionality of the fairness doctrine itself in the courts. Rather, as *Broadcasting* said, "it had provided a formidable brief, which included relevant case citations, for anyone else wanting to do so."[200]

Fowler, in a released statement, said the commission's report was an "indictment" of a "misguided" government policy. He continued, "Today's order is a statement by this commission that we should reverse course and head ballistically toward liberty of the press for radio and television. Free speech and free government thrive together or they fail together."[201]

The decision was mistakenly viewed as an affirmation by public interest groups. Andrew Schwartzman of MAP said it was "a big victory" because the commission was "unable to do what they wanted to do, which was throw it out."[202] Commission opponents in Congress also misjudged the documents ultimate impact. Thomas Rogers, senior counsel to House Telecommunications Subcommittee, said of the commission's findings, "Obviously, we have a disagreement with the Commission on the merits of the fairness doctrine." He continued, "All the Commission action amounts to is making a recommendation to Congress. I feel very comfortable saying from the House perspective that this is one Commission recommendation that isn't likely to get any action here."[203]

On the same day the commission released its Fairness Report, the *Washington Post* was speculating on Fowler's successor. Despite the fact that chairman Fowler's term did not expire until 1986, "Several people are eyeing the chairmanship of the FCC," the *Post* claimed.[204]

It named Dennis Patrick and Mimi Weyforth Dawson as rumored top contenders.[205] But the *Post* also cited an unnamed source close to Fowler saying he was now open to reappointment. "He has announced to several people he is toying with the idea," the *Post's* source said.[206] Fowler himself said, "I have a three-word comment: Premature, I hope."[207]

But resignation was not premature for Henry Rivera. He ended months of speculation by announcing his resignation at the beginning of open agenda meeting August 7. He said he would leave the FCC, effective September 15, to join Dow, Lohnes & Albertson, a communications law firm.[208] Speculation began immediately on who would replace what *Television Digest* described as Rivera's "moderating influence." Subcommittee Chairman Wirth (D-Colorado) said the commission was "losing a staunch defender of the public's interest."[209]

Television Digest said that a replacement for Rivera would not come quickly. It said the "FCC is expected to operate short one member for weeks or even months."[210] Citing unnamed Administration sources, it said that "there's no front-runner as Rivera successor and that none of the early candidates is likely to get nod."[211] These early candidates included Edwin Lavergne, 31, communications attorney at Washington law firm Finely, Kumble, Wagner, Heine, Underberg, Manley & Casey; Representative Leland's legislative director, Larry Irving; and Derrick Humphries of Washington law firm Brown & Finn.[212] Other early candidates were Steven Pena, a lawyer with Gurman, Kurtis & Blask, an offshoot of Becker, Gurman, Lucas, O'Brien & Raison; and Louis McCarren, chairman of Vermont Public Service Board.[213]

Friday, September 13, Radio and Television News Director Association (RTNDA) members adopted a resolution calling on the Association "to initiate and fully prosecute judicial proceedings" to repeal the fairness doctrine. Interestingly, at the same time RTNDA also adopted a resolution commending the FCC on its report to Congress calling Section 315 of the Communications Act and the fairness doctrine "not in the public interest."[214]

Mark Fowler, Tuesday, September 25, in a speech before the International Radio Television Society,[215] in New York, titled "The General of New Choice," identified what he considered to be the perfect metaphor to describe his 'unregulation' campaign. Again, advancing what he saw as the need for a print model for broadcasting, he explained how his 'unregulation' plan had achieved unthought of positive results. In searching for the "apt metaphor for this," he said he was struck with it when "I went to make some popcorn and hauled out one of those new hot air poppers. Unlike older machines, these poppers require no oil. They pop corn with hot air."[216] He then went on to explain:

> The amazing thing about this machine is that it produces so much popcorn, far more than it appears that it can handle. And it produces it all without the use of what was long thought to be a necessary ingredient of the process, oil.
>
> In many ways, this device describes the deregulatory principle of the FCC's policy. Remove what was thought an essential ingredient--heavy government regulation--and our communications system works; in fact, it works better. I call this principle the Popcorn Principle.[217]

Did this mean he replaced the government hot oil with his own hot air?

Television Digest, on October 7, identified three more potential candidates to succeed ex-commissioner Rivera. The latest three were Walter Threadgill, Storer Communications corporate vice president in Washington; Drew Pettus, attorney and administrative assistant to Representative Swift (D-Washington); and Joseph Guzman of GTE Sprint.[218]

With RTNDA leading the way, several print and broadcast organizations challenged the constitutionality of the fairness doctrine in a filing, Monday, October 21, in the U.S. Appeals Court, District of Columbia.[219] The groups maintained the doctrine was in violation of the first amendment, "and is otherwise arbitrary and capricious and contrary to law." The filing asked that the doctrine be "set aside, modified or reversed."

The appeal was based on the August 7, FCC Fairness Doctrine Report, which found the doctrine "constitutionally suspect," "chills" free speech, and no longer was necessary because the number of media outlets for public expression had grown substantially since the *Red Lion* decision in 1969 affirming the doctrine.[220]

RTNDA President John Spain, news director of WBRZ Baton Rouge, was quoted by *Television Digest* as saying:

> The FCC erred in following the logic of its own findings about the chilling effects of the doctrine and the increasing diversity of the media in the marketplace of ideas. The Commission should have determined that the fairness doctrine is not mandated by the Communications Act. The FCC then should have moved to repeal the doctrine, which it found deserves the public interest.[221]

RTNDA announced that CBS "will be the major contributor" to the court effort, and Timothy Dyk of the network's Washington law firm Wilmer, Cutler & Pickering had prepared the appeal. Besides RTNDA and CBS, others included as plaintiffs in the petition were the NAB, NRBA, Gaylord Broadcasting Co., Post-Newsweek Co., Tribune Broadcasting Col, Gannet Co. and Meredith Corp.[222]

As *Broadcasting* said of the appeal on October 21, "The petition for review appears to have the seeds of a court battle that could reach the Supreme Court. One question the challenge posed was who will defend the doctrine. Given its criticism of the doctrine, some felt the FCC may not be in a position to perform that function."[223]

There was no comment on this from the commission. It claimed it was "not even aware the petition is to be filed." It said it "could not say what the agency's position would be."[224] There were others aware of RTNDA's appeal, though. Fifteen individuals and groups filed to have the RTNDA appeal dismissed. They claimed the commission report the appeal was based on was not ready for court review because the report did not constitute a final action.

In the last week of October, the commission made formal what had in the past year already become the practice. It announced it would hold less frequent public meetings. When Fowler assumed the chair of the commission in 1981, he promised more frequent and more open meetings. Now, in announcing there would be only three more meetings for the rest of the year, also came an announcement that a large majority of items would be acted on by circulation to commissioners, without public notice.

The less frequent meeting schedule was claimed to be part of a plan by Jerald Fritz, Chairman Fowler's chief of staff, "to make the Commission operations more efficient."[225] Fritz, in an interview with *Television Digest*, said "Commission efficiency will improve with fewer meetings by speeding the process." He also said that most items on circulation were "noncontroversial."[226]

In a speech before a joint meeting of the ABA Forum Committee on Communications Law, and the Federal Communications Bar Association, in Washington the third week of November, Quello said:

> We should remember that the laws and regulations which govern broadcasting have recognized that it is a form of commerce requiring extraordinary oversight by government. That it is not just another commercial enterprise is quite evident when you consider provisions of the Communications Act, particularly Sections 315 and 312(1)(7). Whether we like it or not the law clearly recognizes broadcasting to be a special case which requires extraordinary government treatment-treatment beyond that accorded to the printed press or any other business.[227]

But then he goes on to say of repealing Section 315 and the fairness doctrine:

> RTNDA is the appropriate organization to spearhead this renewed campaign. Courts are the logical vehicles for Constitutional challenge.[228]

Later the same week, speaking before a Hofstra University television conference in Hempstead, New York, Quello called for the implementation of "a practical spectrum usage fee" on broadcasters in return for "clean, decisive legislative surgery" to remove first amendment and regulatory constraints from the Communications Act.[229] He also reiterated his call to broadcasters, and the RTNDA, for a more emphatic lobbying effort before Congress for their first amendment rights.[230] Quello singled out the fairness doctrine as particularly in need of elimination. He urged broadcasters to "get off their seats, and sell something more important than broadcast time."[231]

The White House Office of Management and Budget notified the commission, October 15, that the information collected under the FCC's political editorializing rule ran counter to the Paperwork Reduction Act. It directed the commission to take steps to amend or eliminate the rule.[232]

The political editorializing rule requires a broadcaster who opposes or endorses a candidate to notify the opposed candidate or the endorsed candidate's opponents of the editorial within 24 hours, to provide scripts or tapes of the editorials, and to offer a reasonable opportunity to respond. *Broadcasting*, citing an OMB letter to the FCC, said that the information collected according to the rule "does not appear to have practical utility that justifies the burden imposed."[233]

The FCC rulemaking launched two years before (Doc. 83-484) proposing to eliminate the political editorializing and personal attack rules was still pending. It had remained inactive since Congress expressed its strong opposition to it in reports accompanying appropriations for the FCC. Congress had directed the commission not to tamper with either rule. *Television Digest* said the FCC responded, November 22, to OMB. It promised to include a reconsideration of station notifications in its pending rulemaking (Doc. 83-484), and that the proceeding was likely to be wrapped up "within weeks."[234]

In December, the Democratic National Committee and Representative John Dingell (D-Michigan), chairman of the House Energy and Commerce Committee, joined other intervenors asking the U.S. Court of Appeals, District of Columbia, to dismiss the Radio-Television News Directors Association's appeal of the FCC fairness doctrine report. The motion said the court should decline review because the commission had referred the matter to Congress. The motion was filed in behalf of the DNC and Dingell by former FCC Chairman Charles D. Ferris.[235]

Also, in December, Meredith announced it had retained additional counsel to argue its case. It announced that Floyd Abrams, of New York, one the nation's leading first amendment lawyers, would be retained as an additional counsel.[236]

Meanwhile, *Television Digest*, citing unnamed congressional sources, said part of the reason it was taking so long for the White House to fill ex-commissioner Rivera's vacant slot on the FCC was that Senate Communications Subcommittee Chairman Goldwater (R-Arizona) was sticking to his choice for post, Derrick Humphries. *Television Digest* also said the Subcommittee's Democrats were pushing hard for a change in length of FCC terms. Reportedly Subcommittee Democrats wanted commissioner terms shortened from seven years to five starting with Fowler's (up next year), and Rivera's vacant seat shortened to 3-4 years. This way, the seats would be open at the start of the next president's term to give the next president (regardless of party, they say) the chance to put his "own people into jobs."[237]

Notes

1984

[1]"NAB turns to FCC for new GC." *Television Digest.* January 16, 1984. 24:3. p.5.

[2]"In brief: Content regulation of radio and television." *Broadcasting.* January 23, 1984. v.106. p.128.

[3]Ibid.

[4]Freedom of Expression Act of 1983, Hearings Before the Committee on Commerce, Science, and Transportation, U.S. Senate, 98th Congress, 2nd Session. On To Provide that the Federal Communications Commission Shall Not Regulate the Content of Certain Communications, January 30, February 1 and 8, 1984, Serial No. 98-62, S. Hrg. 98-681.

[5]William F. Chamberlain, Ph.D., Associate Professor, School of Journalism, University of North Carolina at Chapel Hill and Willard D. Rowland, Jr., Ph.D., Assistant Professor, Institute for Communications Research, University of Illinois, Urbana-Champaign.

[6]Freedom of Expression Act of 1983, Hearings Before the Committee on Commerce, Science, and Transportation, U.S. Senate, 98th Congress, 2nd Session. On To Provide that the Federal Communications Commission Shall Not Regulate the Content of Certain Communications, January 30, February 1 and 8, 1984, Serial No. 98-62, S. Hrg. 98-681.

[7]Ibid., at p.70.

[8]Ibid.

[9]Ibid.

[10]Ibid. They cite as an example: Michael Schudson, *Discovering the News: A Social History of American Newspapers* (New York: Basic Books, 1978). At p.64.

[11]Ibid., at p.71.

[12]Ibid.

[13]Ibid., at pp.71-2.

[14]Ibid., at p.72. They cite as examples within the scholarly literature two particularly insightful discussions: Fred Friendly, *The Good Guys, the Bad Guys and the First Amendment: Free Speech vs. Fairness in Broadcasting* (New York: Vintage, 1977); and Benno C. Schmidt, Jr., *Freedom of the Press vs. Public Access* (New York: Praeger, 1976).

[15]Ibid. They cite as examples remarks delivered by Daniel L. Ritchie, Chairman and Chief Executive Officer of Group W, Westinghouse Broadcasting and Cable, Inc., as part of the First Annual Everett Parker Lecture on Ethics in Telecommunications in New York City on September 9, 1983. He argues there that responsible broadcasters are already in effect meeting or exceeding the content regulations and that their elimination could actually work against stations' ability to maintain such service.

[16]Ibid.

[17]Ibid.

[18]Ibid., at p.73. Here they cite treatments of two separate, but ultimately closely interrelated control streams of communications regulatory and legislative policy activity; see Willard D. Rowland, Jr., "The process of reification: Recent trends in communications legislation and policy-making," *Journal of Communications*, Autumn 1982, 32:4; pp.114-136; and Dan Schiller, *Telematics and Government* (Norwood, N.J.: Ablex, 1982).

[19]Ibid.

[20]Ibid., at p.73. They suggest for a discussion of these issues see: Theodore Glasser, "Competition and diversity among radio formats: Legal and structural issues," *Journal of Broadcasting*; Don R. LeDuc, "Deregulation and the dream of diversity," *Journal of Communication*, Autumn 1982, 32:4, pp.164-176; and U.S. House, Committee on Energy and Commerce, Subcommittee on Telecommunications, Consumer Protection and Finance, "Telecommunications in Transition: The Status of Competition in the Telecommunications Industry." Majority Staff Report, 97th Congress, 1st Session, November 3, 1981.

[21]Ibid., at p.74. They suggested noting recent industry representations on the principle of public ownership of the spectrum, as in U.S. House, Committee on Energy and Commerce, Subcommittee on Telecommunications, Consumer Protection, and Finance, "Broadcast Reform Proposals." Hearing, 97th Congress, 1st Session, November 3, 1981, especially pp.121 ff. and subsequent NAB correspondence with the subcommittee.

[22]Ibid.

[23]"FCC grilled at House oversight hearing." *Television Digest*. February 13, 1984. 24:7. pp.3-4. At p.3.

[24]Hearing Before the Subcommittee on Telecommunications, Consumer Protection, and Finance of the Committee on Energy and Commerce, U.S. House of Representatives, 98th Congress, 2nd Session. FCC Oversight. Serial No. 98-106. February 8, 1985.

> See also: Hearing Before the Subcommittee on Telecommunications, Consumer Protection, and Finance of the Committee on Energy and Commerce, U.S. House of Representatives, 98th Congress, 2nd Session. On H.R. 6122, H.R.

6134. Broadcast Regulation and Station Ownership. Serial No. 98-176. September 19, 1984.

[25]Ibid., at pp.1-2.

[26]Ibid., at p.35.

[27]"The Fifth Estate's freedom fighter." *Broadcasting*. February 13, 1984. v.106. p.188,190,192,194. At p.190.

[28]Ibid.

[29]Ibid., at p.192.

[30]Ibid.

[31]"FCC postpones fairness inquiry." *Broadcasting*. February 27, 1984. v.106. p.35.

[32]Ibid.

[33]"Fowler scolded at session." *Television Digest*. March 26, 1984. 24:13. p.4.

[34]Ibid.

[35]Ibid.

[36]Nomination-Federal Communications Commission, Hearing Before the Committee on Commerce, Science, and Transportation, U.S. Senate, 98th Congress, 2nd Session. On Nomination of Dennis R. Patrick, To be Be a Member, Federal Communications Commission, March 26, 1984, S. Hrg. 98-740. At p. 1.

[37]Ibid., at p.2.

[38]Ibid.

[39]Ibid.

[40]Ibid., at p.11.

[41]Ibid.

[42]Ibid.

[43]Ibid., at p.12.

[44]Ibid.

[45]Ibid.

[46]Ibid.

[47]Ibid., at p.13.

[48]"Patrick cleared by Senate committee for FCC seat." *Broadcasting*. April 2, 1984. v.106. p.68.

[49]"FCC's Patrick: Emerging independent. *Broadcasting*. April 9, 1984. v.106. pp.76,78. At p.76.

[50]Ibid.

[51]Inquiry Into Section 73.910 of the Commission's Rules and Regulations concerning the General Fairness Doctrine Obligations of Broadcast Licensees. Gen. Docket No. 84-282, 49 Fed. Reg. 20317 (May 14, 1984).

[52]"FCC inquiry to assess fairness doctrine." *Television Digest*. April 16, 1984. 24:16. pp.1-2. At p.1.

[53]Ibid., at p.2.

[54]Ibid.

[55]Ibid.

[56]Ibid.

[57]"Words of warning on fairness." *Broadcasting*. April 23, 1984. v.106. p.38.

[58]Ibid.

[59]"Mark Fowler's great experiment: Setting his people free." *Broadcasting*. April 30, 1984. v.106. p.116(7). At p.118.

[60]Ibid., at p.120.

[61]Ibid., at p.128.

[62]Ibid.

[63]"NAB report: Dereg drive brakes at D.C. crossroads." Paul Harris. *Variety*. May 2, 1984. v.315. p.130.

[64]"Fowler raps broadcasters." *Television Digest*. May 7, 1984. 24:19. pp.6-7. At p.6.

[65]Ibid., at pp.6-7.

[66]Ibid., at p.6.

[67]Ibid.

[68]Inquiry Into Section 73.910 of the Commission's Rules and Regulations concerning the General Fairness Doctrine Obligations of Broadcast Licensees. Gen. Docket No. 84-282, 49 Fed. Reg. 20317 (May 14, 1984).

[69]"FCC releases fairness doctrine notice of inquiry." *Broadcasting*. May 14, 1984. v.106. pp.70,72. At p.70.

[70]"Lack of quorum stalls movement on Packwood's FEA." *Broadcasting*. May 14, 1984. v.106. p.76.

[71]"Nomination of James Henry Quello to be a member of the Federal Communications Commission." Ronald Reagan. *Public Papers of the Presidents: Ronald Reagan: 1984*. U.S. Government Printing Office. Washington: 1986. May 15, 1984. p.702.

[72]"It's go again for Quello at the FCC." *Broadcasting*. May 21, 1984. v.106. p.38.

[73]"NAB studies fairness doctrine." *Television Digest*. June 4, 1984. 24:23. p.10.

[74]Ibid.

[75]Ibid.

[76]Nominations--June, Hearings Before the Committee on Commerce, Science, and Transportation, U.S. Senate, 98th Congress, 2nd Session. On June 7, 1984, Nomination of James H. Quello, To Be a Member of the Federal Communications Commission, Serial No. 98-97, S. Hrg. 98-983.

[77]Ibid., at p.35.

[78]Ibid., at pp.36-7.

[79]Ibid., at p.44.

[80]Ibid.

[81]Ibid., at pp.45-6.

[82]"Quello closes in on another term." *Broadcasting.* June 11, 1984. v.106. p.46.

[83]"Shaping the law with a Fein touch." *Broadcasting.* June 11, 1984. v.106. p.111.

[84]Ibid.

[85]Ibid.

[86]Ibid.

[87]Ibid.

[88]Report and Order in MM Docket No. 83-670, 98 FCC 2d 1076 (1984) (Television Deregulation).

[89]"FCC deregulates commercial TV." *Television Digest.* July 2, 1984. 24:27. pp.1-3. At p.1.

[90]Ibid., at p.2.

[91]Ibid.

[92]"Deregulation comes to television: FCC in unanimous vote follows pattern of radio dereg for commercial and public TV." *Broadcasting.* July 2, 1984. v.107. pp.31-2. At p.31.

[93]Ibid., at p.32.

[94]Ibid.

[95]Ibid.

[96]"Party-line reaction to FCC vote to K.O. more TV regs." *Variety.* July 4, 1984. v.315. p.53.

[97]Ibid.

[98]*FCC v. League of Women Voters of California,* 468 U.S. 364 (1984).

[99]"High court notes dereg interest." *Television Digest.* July 9, 1984. 24:28. pp.2-3. At p.2.

[100]Ibid.

[101]Ibid., at pp.2-3.

[102]"Two tails that could wag the dog in winning First Amendment rights." *Broadcasting.* July 9, 1984. v.107. p.27(3). At p.27.

[103]Ibid.

[104]"High court notes dereg interest." *Television Digest.* July 9, 1984. 24:28. pp.2-3. At p.3.

[105]Ibid.

[106]Ibid.

[107]Ibid.

[108]"Two tails that could wag the dog in winning First Amendment rights." *Broadcasting.* July 9, 1984. v.107. p.27(3). At p.27.

[109]Ibid.

[110]Ibid.

[111]Ibid., at p.29.

[112]"Why TV is being freed from 'heavy hand of government'." *U.S. News & World Report.* July 23, 1984. v.97. pp.47-8. At p.47.

[113]Ibid., at p.48.

[114]"McKinney raps broadcasters." *Television Digest.* August 20, 1984. 24:34. p.6.

[115]Ibid.

[116]"McKinney urges broadcasters to fight hard on fairness doctrine." *Broadcasting.* August 20, 1984. v.107. pp.51-2. At p.52.

[117]"Mass Media Bureau's mover and shaker." *Broadcasting.* August 27, 1984. v.107. p.143.

[118]Ibid.

[119]Ibid.

[120]"No surprises in fairness doctrine comments." *Television Digest.* September 10, 1984. 24:37. pp.3-4. At p.3.

[121]Ibid.

[122]Ibid., at p.4.

[123]"FCC urged to repeal fairness doctrine." *Broadcasting.* September 10, 1984. v.107. pp.37-8. At p.37.

[124]Ibid.

[125]"No surprises in fairness doctrine comments." *Television Digest.* September 10, 1984. 24:37. pp.3-4.

[126]"Fowler to shift Hill liaison." *Television Digest.* October 1, 1984. 24:40. p.5.

[127]Complaint of Syracuse Peace Council against Television Station WTVH, 99 FCC 2d 1389, 57 Rad. Reg. 2d (P&F) 519 (1984), recon. denied, 59 Rad Reg. 2d (P&F) 179 (1985).

See generally: Syracuse Peace Council, FCC 84-518 (released December 20, 1984), 57 RR 2d 519 (1984).

[128]"FCC upholds fairness doctrine complaint." *Television Digest.* October 29, 1984. 24:34. pp.1-2. At p.1.

[129]"FCC finds first fairness violation since Fowler." *Broadcasting.* October 29, 1984. v.107. p.34.

[130]Ibid.

[131]Video tape of FCC commission meeting, October 26, 1984.

[132]"Items on the move." *Broadcasting.* October 29, 1984. v.107. p.34.

[133]"Lost in fairness land." *Broadcasting.* November 5, 1984. v.107. p.106.

[134]Ibid.

[135]"Report to the Chairman' on commission's fourth year accomplishments." Edward J. Minkel. *Television-Radio Age.* September 16 1985. v.33. pp.101-2. At p.102.

---

[136]"Communications report: Fowler's FCC learns some hard lessons about what it means to be 'independent'." Ann Cooper. *National Journal.* April 6, 1985. pp.732-6. At p.734.

[137]"FCC's Dennis Patrick: In the communications pipeline." *Broadcasting.* December 10, 1984. v.107. p.119.

[138]Ibid.

[139]Ibid.

[140]Ibid.

1985

[141]"CIA's fairness complaint denied." *Television Digest.* January 14, 1985. 25:2. pp.3-4. At p.4.

[142]*Central Intelligence Agency v. ABC, Inc.*, 57 Rad. Reg. 2d (P&F) 1543 (Mass Media Bur.), aff'd, 58 Rad. Reg. 2d (P&F) 1544 (1985).

[143]"CIA's fairness complaint denied." *Television Digest.* January 14, 1985. 25:2. pp.3-4. At p.3.

[144]S.22, 99th Congress, 1st Session (1985).

[145]Ibid., at pp.3-4.

[146]*CBS, Inc.*, 95 FCC 2d 1152 (1983).

[147]"Is fairness doctrine codified in legislation?" *Television Digest.* February 11, 1985. 25:6. pp.3-5. At p.5.

Besides Dingle, the group also included Norman Lear, Embassy Television; Erwin Griswold, (who as U.S. solicitor general successfully defended the fairness doctrine when it was challenged before the Supreme Court in 1969 in *Red Lion Broadcasting Co. vs. FCC*); Esther Peterson, representative, International Organization of Consumers Unions, United Nations; Mario Obledo, League of United Latin American Citizens; Dorothy Ridings, League of Women Voters, and Mary Futrell, National Education Association.

Among the 17 organizations participating in the Campaign for Free Speech coalition were: the Telecommunications Research and Action Center, the Media Access Project, the American Civil Liberties Union, the American Lung Association, Black Citizens for a Fair Media, Consumers Union, the Consumer Federation of America, the National Organization for Women Legal Defense and Educational Fund, People for the American Way, the United Auto Workers, the United Church of Christ and the United States Public Interest Research Group.

[148]"Coalition formed to fight for retention of fairness doctrine." *Broadcasting*. February 11, 1985. v.108. p.61.

[149]"FCC's fairness hearings look like another rerun." Paul Harris. *Variety*. February 13, 1985. v.318. p.117.

[150]"Is fairness doctrine codified in legislation?" *Television Digest*. February 11, 1985. 25:6. pp.3-5. At p.5.

[151]Ibid., at p.3.

[152]"The great debate on fairness is a little less than that." *Broadcasting*. February 11, 1985. v.108. pp.30-2. At p.31.

[153]"Is fairness doctrine codified in legislation?" *Television Digest*. February 11, 1985. 25:6. pp.3-5. At p.3.

[154]"The great debate on fairness is a little less than that." *Broadcasting*. February 11, 1985. v.108. pp.30-2. At p.31.

[155]"FCC urged to abolish its 'Fairness Doctrine'." Michael Isikoff. *The Washington Post*. February 8, 1985.

[156]"The great debate on fairness is a little less than that." *Broadcasting*. February 11, 1985. v.108. pp.30-2. At p.32.

[157]"FCC's fairness hearings look like another rerun." Paul Harris. *Variety*. February 13, 1985. v.318. p.117.

[158]"The bittersweet chairmanship of Mark S. Fowler." *Broadcasting*. February 18, 1985. 108:7. pp.39-41. At p.39.

[159]Ibid.

[160]Ibid., at p.40.

[161]Ibid.

[162]Ibid.

[163]"Quotations from the chairman." *Broadcasting*. February 18, 1985. 108:7. pp.41-3. At p.41.

[164]Ibid., at p.43.

[165]Address Before the National Telephone Cooperative Association. February 26, 1985. In "The Federal Communications Commission 1981-1987: What the chairman said." *Hastings COMM/ENT Law Journal*. Winter 1988. Vol. 10. pp.409-500. At p.415.

[166]"FCC comr. Patrick." *Television Digest*. March 11, 1985. 25:10. p.5.

[167]Reauthorization and Oversight of the FCC, Hearing before the Subcommittee on Communications, of the Committee on Commerce, Science, and Transportation, U.S. Senate, 99th Congress, 1st Session. On Reauthorization and Oversight of the Federal Communications Commission, March 20, 1985, S. Hrg. 99-66.

[168]Ibid., at p.2.

[169]Ibid.

[170]Ibid., at p.3.

[171]Ibid., at p.50.

[172]*FCC v. League of Women Voters of California*, 468 U.S. 364 (1984).

[173]"Fairness doctrine probed." *Television Digest*. April 1, 1985. 25:13. p.7.

[174]"Fairness relief, if any, to come from courts." *Broadcasting*. April 8, 1985. v.108. p.142.

[175]Ibid.

[176]"Thirteen staffers identified as major influences at FCC; commissioners applaud contributions of oldtimers and some newer faces." *Television-Radio Age*. April 15, 1985. v.32. pp.55(4). At p.212.

[177]"WTVH seeks fairness review." *Television Digest*. April 15, 1985. 25:15. p.9.

[178]"What's new at the FCC: Fairness doctrine, deregulation and daytimers among topics discussed by FCC commissioners, staff." *Broadcasting*. April 22, 1985. v.107. pp.58,62. At p.58.

[179]"Inside the FCC: Rivera seeks to leave agency." Elizabeth Tucker. *The Washington Post*. April 23, 1985.

[180]Ibid.

[181]"Fowler seeks auction bill." *Television Digest*. May 6, 1985. 25:18. p.7.

[182]"Nomination of Dennis R. Patrick to be a member of the Federal Communications Commission." Ronald Reagan. *Public Papers of the Presidents: Ronald Reagan: 1985*. U.S. Government Printing Office. Washington: 1987. May 30, 1985. pp.698-9.

[183]Hearings Before the Committee on Commerce, Science, and Transportation, U.S. Senate, 99th Congress, 1st Session. On July 11, 1985, Nomination of Dennis Patrick, to be a Commissioner, Federal Communications Commission, S. Hrg. 99-344. pp.1-17.

[184]"Patrick sails through friendly confirmation hearing in Senate." *Broadcasting*. July 15, 1985. v.109. p.34.

[185]Hearings Before the Committee on Commerce, Science, and Transportation, U.S. Senate, 99th Congress, 1st Session. On July 11, 1985, Nomination of Dennis Patrick, to be a Commissioner, Federal Communications Commission, S. Hrg. 99-344. At p.16.

[186]Ibid.

[187]Ibid.

[188]"Has the FCC gone too far? Even fans of deregulation say chairman Fowler is rushing things." John Wilke, Mark Vamos and Mark Maremont. *Business Week*. August 5, 1985. pp.48-54. At p.51.

[189]Ibid.

[190]Ibid., at p.54.

[191]Inquiry Into Section 73.1910 of the Commission's Rules and Regulations Concerning Alternatives to the General Fairness Doctrine Obligations of Broadcast Licensees. Gen Docket No. 84-282, 102 FCC 2d 145 (1985) ("1985 Fairness Report").

[192]"Fairness doctrine: The FCC doesn't like it but says it will be enforced." *Broadcasting*. August 12, 1985. v.109. pp.30-31. At p.30.

[193]"FCC offers ammo for fairness challenge." *Broadcasting*. August 26, 1985. v.109. p.38.

[194]1985 Fairness Report. At p.147.

[195]Ibid., at p.148.

[196]Ibid.

[197]Ibid, at p.247.

[198]Ibid.

[199]Ibid.

[200]"FCC offers ammo for fairness challenge." *Broadcasting*. August 26, 1985. v.109. p.38.

[201]"Fairness doctrine: The FCC doesn't like it but says it will be enforced." *Broadcasting*. August 12, 1985. v.109. pp.30-31.

[202]"FCC offers 'indictment' of fairness doctrine." *Television Digest*. August 12, 1985. 25:32. pp.1-2. At p.2.

[203]Ibid.

[204]"Inside the FCC: Several seeking chairman's job." *The Washington Post*. August 7, 1985.

[205]Ibid.

[206]Ibid.

[207]Ibid.

[208]"Rivera resigns from FCC." *Television Digest*. August 12, 1985. 25:32. p.4.

[209]Ibid.

[210]"No front-runner for Rivera seat." *Television Digest*. September 16, 1985. 25:37. p.6.

[211]Ibid.

[212]"Rivera resigns from FCC." *Television Digest*. August 12, 1985. 25:32. p.4.

[213]"No front-runner for Rivera seat." *Television Digest*. September 16, 1985. 25:37. p.6.

[214]"RTNDA has 'momentum,' plans expansion." *Television Digest*. September 16, 1985. 25:37. pp.1-3. At p.1.

[215]Speech Before the International Radio Television Society: "The General of New Choice." September 24, 1985. New York, New York. In "The Federal Communications Commission 1981-1987: What the chairman said." *Hastings COMM/ENT Law Journal*. Winter 1988. Vol. 10. pp.409-500. At pp.427-8,443.

[216]Ibid., at p.427.

[217]Ibid.

[218]"Threadgill among FCC candidates." *Television Digest*. October 7, 1985. 25:40. p.6.

[219]*Radio-Television News Directors Association v. Federal Communications Commission*, 809 F.2d 860, vacated. 831 F.2d (D.C. Cir. 1987), pet. for review dismissed as moot, Order, No. 85-1691 (D.C. Cir. Nov. 3, 1987).

[220]"RTNDA leads court challenge to fairness doctrine." *Television Digest*. October 21, 1985. 25:42. pp.1-2. At p.1.

[221]Ibid., at p.2.

[222]"Broadcasters go after fairness doctrine." *Broadcasting*. October 21, 1985. v.109. p.39.

[223]Ibid.

[224]Ibid.

[225]"FCC item circulations questioned." *Television Digest*. October 28, 1985. 25:43. p.4.

[226]Ibid.

[227]"Technology explosion, deregulation provide many new challenges." James H. Quello. *Television-Radio Age*. November, 25, 1985. v.33. pp.109-10. At p.110.

[228]Ibid.

[229]"Quello refloats trial balloon on spectrum fees." *Broadcasting*. November 25, 1985. v.109. pp.35-6. At p.35.

[230]Ibid.

[231]Ibid., at p36.

[232]"FCC's political editorializing rule challenged." *Broadcasting*. November 25, 1985. v.109. p.60.

[233]Ibid.

[234]"OMB hits FCC editorial rules." *Television Digest*. November 25, 1985. 25:47. p.5.

[235]"DNC, Dingell want dismissal of RTNDA appeal of FCC fairness doctrine report." *Broadcasting*. December 23, 1985. v.109. pp.57-8. At p.58.

[236]Ibid.

[237]"Joyce's job seen on line." *Television Digest*. December 23, 1985. 25:51. p.6.

CHAPTER V

PRESENTED THE OPPORTUNITY THE FCC AXES FAIRNESS, 1986-1987

A number of events occurred in 1986 and 1987 which provided the commission the opportunities it needed to finally rid itself of the fairness doctrine. But some of these defining events were not as spontaneous as the commission presented them. They were more a result of the record the commission itself built between 1981 and 1985.

1986

There were three particularly significant events relative to the fairness doctrine which highlight 1986. First, Mark Fowler was renominated by Reagan. This can be viewed as a sign of continued Administration approval of his 'unregulation' policies. It also meant the commission would continue to pursue, with the means at its disposal, ridding itself of the fairness doctrine. The other two significant events of 1986 were even more directly related to the fairness doctrine. Meredith and RTNDA took up the commission's own challenge to use its findings to challenge the doctrine in court. The final event directly related to the fairness doctrine was to prove the *deus ex machina* the commission had been looking for. It came from an totally unexpected determination by the U.S. Court of Appeals, District of Columbia, in TRAC's appeal of the commission's 1983 teletext determination. In writing the panel opinion in the *TRAC* appeal, Judge Robert Bork stated the fairness doctrine was not codified. And as such, he said, the commission could act to remove it without congressional action.

On January 13, 1986, *Television Digest*,[1] ran a story saying that White House officials had confirmed that Administration labor lawyer, Patricia Diaz Dennis, 39, was Reagan's "tentative selection" to succeed Henry Rivera on the commission. Dennis, an Albuquerque native like Rivera, was also a Democrat. She was currently a member of the National Labor Relations board. Dennis acknowledged that she was under consideration for the FCC opening. *Broadcasting*, reported that Dennis had voted for Reagan, and she was identified as a Reagan supporter.[2]

By the third and fourth week of January, respectively, the commission had to come up with a consistent position in two seemingly contradictory cases. The *DNC* had its initial court hearing the third week of January, and *Meredith* had its initial court hearing the fourth week. The Democratic National Committee, and other citizen groups, had filed to dismiss the appeal that RTNDA had taken from the commission's 1985 Fairness Doctrine Report.[3] In this case, the FCC was the respondent. And it chose to side with RTNDA, whose aim was to have fairness declared unconstitutional.[4] In the hearing, DNC argued that the RTNDA appeal was premature since the commission's Report did not take a final action. But the commission, siding with RTNDA and the media groups, argued its 1985 Fairness Report was, as the commission put it, "a final agency action that is reviewable at this time."[5] The RTNDA appeal drew heavily on the commission's findings in its Report. And it sought to persuade the court to declare the doctrine unconstitutional. RTNDA pointed out that the commission had already publicly stated it hoped a court would declare it unconstitutional.

The Meredith Corp., in its arguments filed the fourth week of January, with the U.S. Court of Appeals, District of Columbia,[6] also claimed that the commission, itself, had provided the signal to challenge the doctrine's constitutionality. What's more, the brief said, the commission had produced the findings on which the court could hold the doctrine was unconstitutional.[7] But rather than side with Meredith in this case, the commission, in its filing, said that rather than acting on its own findings, it would defer to the courts and to Congress. This was a weak position, at best. And FCC general counsel, Jack Smith, acknowledged this situation was "unusual" in a January 27, *Broadcasting*, interview.[8]

Meredith's constitutional arguments challenging the doctrine relied heavily on the benchmark, 1974 Supreme Court newspaper decision, *Miami Herald Publishing Co. v. Tornillo.*[9] The Court held in *Miami Herald* that a Florida state law, similar to the fairness doctrine, was a violation of the first amendment.[10] Meredith's 56-page brief also emphasized that the commission's 1985 Fairness Report eliminated whatever rationale had existed for according broadcast journalists less first amendment protection than print journalists.[11]

The question whether the commission would adequately represent the government's interest in these cases was not lost on certain members of Congress. House Telecommunications Subcommittee Chairman Wirth (D-Colorado), also questioned the ability of the U.S. Appeals Court, District of Columbia, to review a challenge to fairness doctrine, when the FCC itself had not acted to modify or repeal the rule. *Television Digest*, reported that Wirth sent a letter to Fowler. Wirth reportedly told Fowler the 1985 Report's conclusions amounted to little more than recommendations to Congress. Wirth said it did not represent a final action on which Court could base a decision.[12] (Recall the announcement of the commission's Inquiry said the purpose was to gather "preliminary" material.)

But Fowler was not ready to back down. Instead, the commission showed its own mindset in the form of a 24-point FCC congressional wish list. This was agreed to by the commissioners at its January 30, meeting. And it was sent to Congress. Not surprisingly, the recommendations included a call to repeal equal time, reasonable access rules, and the fairness doctrine. These recommendations were virtually identical to the ones the commission had recommend to Congress in 1981.

After months of speculation, and delay, it seemed as though Patricia Diaz Dennis had emerged as an acceptable replacement for Democrat, Henry Rivera, on the commission. But *Broadcasting*, citing a Senate Communications Subcommittee source, said that Democrats would "not allow any new commissioner to be named" until the terms of all FCC commissioners were reduced from seven years to five years. The rationale given was the reduction in term would insure that the Senate had the opportunity to oversee nominations every year. The move had obvious political overtones. Senate Democrats were hoping to gain majority control from the Republicans in November. With Democratic control they would have more say about which nominees got confirmed.[13]   At this time, there was even an outside chance a Democrat would successfully take the presidency.

The first week of March the RTNDA, along with ten other petitioners, presented their challenge to the constitutionality of the FCC's fairness doctrine. They presented in the U.S. Court of Appeals, District of Columbia. RTNDA argued that the fairness doctrine must be considered in light of first amendment principles applicable to broadcast and print journalists alike. On that basis, the petition said, "the doctrine must be judged a violation of the First Amendment."[14] RTNDA's brief had also been filed in the *Meredith* case.

Legislation to shorten FCC commissioner terms from seven years to five years was unanimously approved by the Senate Commerce Committee at a mark-up on Thursday, March 16.[15]   Passage in both Houses was expected, and *Television Digest* reported Reagan was expected to sign the legislation.[16]

Democrats claimed part of the problem was the result of the 1982 congressional action that reduced number of commissioners to five from seven. They claimed it did so without adjusting terms. It is interesting that the 1979 GAO report cited by Congress reducing the number of commissioners had also recommended the length of the terms of commissioners should be increased to 12 years. The GAO report said this would isolate the commission from excessive political tinkering. Now the Senate, through its confirmation process, wanted to increase further its oversight of the FCC.

On Thursday, March 27, the full Senate passed S-2179 (S.Rept. 99-262) to reduce commissioner terms. The legislation was then sent to the House.

On Tuesday, March 11, 1986, President Reagan announced his intention to nominate Patricia Diaz Dennis to the FCC. She would take the Democratic FCC seat vacated by Henry Rivera, and she would serve for the unexpired term of seven year from July 1, 1980.[17]

Assured Reagan would sign the term reduction legislation, the Senate scheduled Patricia Diaz Dennis' nomination hearing for Wednesday, April 9.[18] Democrat Dennis, in her opening statement at the hearing, said her overall philosophy was "to limit governmental regulation to that appropriate to achieve the statutory goals."[19]   In a manner akin to Fowler's statement that the public's interest determining the public interest, she said, "In this manner, the intended beneficiaries of the regulation can participate in determining for themselves what is in their own best interests."[20]

In answer to post-hearing questions submitted by Senator Goldwater, asking whether she believed the commission should have the power regulate the content of television, she replied:

> Whether the Commission should have the power to regulate the content of television is a very complex question. Because it raises significant constitutional issues as well as issues under the Communications Act, I believe the Commission should proceed cautiously with any regulation affecting freedom of speech. The Commission must give due weight to the First Amendment rights, as defined by the courts, in making its public interest determination.[21]

And in response to post-hearing questions submitted by Senator Hollings, asking her views on the proper role the FCC should play with respect to the fairness doctrine and equal time rule, she replied:

> The Fairness Doctrine and the Equal Time Rule affect the exercise of First Amendment rights. I believe the Commission should proceed cautiously with any regulation affecting freedom of speech. As the court have recognized, the public interest standard which guides the Commission necessarily invites reference to First Amendment principles. I am aware that the Commission has submitted a Fairness Report to Congress and that the constitutionality of the Fairness Doctrine is the subject of pending litigation before the U.S. Court of Appeals for the District of Columbia. Until I have an opportunity to carefully examine the record in the underlying FCC proceeding, I am not prepared to come to any conclusions about the Fairness Doctrine. Similarly, I cannot comment on the First Amendment implications of the Equal Time Rule until I have throughly [sic] examined the issue. Both the Fairness Doctrine and the Equal Time Rule are currently in effect. Absent some change in status, I fully intend to enforce both the statute and the Commission's rules embodying them.[22]

The Senate Commerce Committee was expected to recommend Dennis' confirmation, but no action would be taken on the nomination until after passage of S-2179. The legislation would also affect her term. Although Reagan had nominated her to fill a term that expired in 1987, S-2179 would extend her term until 1989.

Fowler's remarks on Wednesday, April 14, at the closing session of the NAB convention, caught many broadcasters by surprise. In usual bold Fowler style, he attacked the public interest standard, and admonished broadcasters for holding on to the public trusteeship concept for regulation.[23] But broadcasters were growing leery. They were increasingly concerned that they were becoming negatively affected by deregulation. And the public trustee concept did offer protection from competition.

The NAB convention also had the usual large number of House and Senate members in attendance. One, Representative Edward J. Markey (D-Massachusetts), was expected to succeed Tim Wirth (D-Colorado), as chairman of the House Telecommunications Subcommittee. Markey's views on broadcasting were not especially well known. At the convention Markey, unlike Fowler, warned broadcasters that "the public interest standard is still in there."[24]

Television Digest reported May 12, that the White House planned to renominate FCC chairman Mark Fowler. Reportedly, Fowler advised the Administration that he wanted to stay in the post. The White House was said to have been pleased with Fowler's decision, and a number of Cabinet members had written the President seeking his reappointment.[25] "The White House is happy to have Fowler stay because he has pushed Reagan deregulatory policy more visibly than any other agency head," *Television Digest* quoted an Administration source as saying.[26] The article also repeated what Fowler had said many times, if he accepted reappointment, he did not expect to stay around for the full term.

The House passed S-2179 on Thursday, May 22.[27] Senate Democrats said they would continue to hold up Patricia Dennis' confirmation until after Reagan signed the legislation.[28]

On Thursday, June 5, 1986, President Reagan officially announced his intention to renominate Mark S. Fowler to be a member of the FCC. Upon confirmation, Fowler would be redesignated chairman.[29]

On Friday, June 6, Reagan signed S-2179 (PL 99-334), reducing FCC commissioner terms to five years.[30] Reagan said, in signing the legislation, that absent congressional action, no commissioner terms would have expired in 1989 or 1990.[31] The Senate Commerce Committee approved Dennis' nomination unanimously on Thursday, June 12.

The third week of June, Fowler's legal adviser, Daniel Brenner, announced his intention to resign on July 12. Brenner had been at the commission seven years. Ferris hired Brenner in 1979 as a legal assistant in the chairman's office. Brenner, a Democrat who had been brought in by Charles Ferris, was able to bridge the gap between Fowler and Ferris. Both Ferris and Fowler were deregulators, but from different perspectives. Ferris wanted to reduce regulation to promote competition. Fowler wanted to cut regulation because he wanted to unshackle business in general.[32]

When interviewed about his resignation by *Television-Radio Age*, Brenner said of Fowler, "I think that both Mark [and me] were committed to trying to make the system of broadcast regulation more rational."[33] With the loss of Brenner, Fowler would not only lose a trusted legal advisor, but he would also lose his speech writer.

The NAB joint board (radio and TV) adopted a policy statement Friday, June 20, calling for the FCC, the courts and Congress to leave broadcasting under the public interest concept of regulation.[34] This action came only two months after Fowler had exhorted broadcasters, at the NAB convention, to rally against this concept. This action illustrated how competition frightened broadcasters more than a potential compromise of their first amendment rights. The vote was unanimous.

The NAB, at the same time, though, reaffirmed its opposition to Section 315 and the fairness doctrine. This resolution said Section 315 and the fairness doctrine were "intrusive, inhibit robust debate, and are premised on a theory of scarcity which has long ceased to exist."[35] This was a good illustration of private interest labeled public interest, according to Fowler's redefinition of the term.

The FCC urged the U.S. Court of Appeals, District of Columbia, to dismiss Meredith Broadcasting Corp.'s appeal of the commission's fairness doctrine complaint against Meredith. The commission chose not to directly address the first amendment issues Meredith raised. The commission, in its brief filed the first week in July, said Meredith had not been injured because of its order. Because on commission reconsideration it had held that Meredith had demonstrated its "good faith in complying with the fairness doctrine." The commission reconsideration concluded no further action against Meredith was warranted. The commission's brief stated its Fairness Report concluded that the fairness doctrine did not serve the public interest and was constitutionally suspect. But, it continued, the appropriate place "to present generalized challenges" to the continuing validity of the doctrine was in the case RTNDA had taken in its appeal from that Report.[36]

Additional provisions added by Senator Ernest Hollings, Thursday, August 14, to appropriations legislation (HR-5161), provide an example of the increasing congressional activity into the operation of the commission. These additional provisions prohibited swaps of commercial and noncommercial VHF and UHF stations, directed the FCC to reconsider its inquiry into the fairness doctrine, and would establish an international telecommunications policy committee in the executive branch.[37]

The fairness provision directed the FCC to reexamine its inquiry into the fairness doctrine "with a complete examination of possible alternative ways of administering and enforcing the fairness doctrine."[38] Hollings said, "In examining this inquiry [1985 Fairness Report] decision, the committee finds that it contains no discussion of possible alternatives to the present scheme of implementing the fairness doctrine so as to maintain its benefits and lower its burdens. The committee considers this a serious weakness in aiding congressional review of the fairness doctrine."[39] The FCC was instructed to submit a report to Congress by September 30, 1987.

Meredith filed its appeal brief the third week of August. It urged the Court of Appeals, District of Columbia, to disregard the FCC's recommendation that its case be dismissed. The brief also contended the fairness doctrine should be thrown out on constitutional grounds.[40]

It started simple enough. The U.S. Court of Appeals, District of Columbia, ruled on September 19, 1986, that the FCC had the power to decide not to apply the fairness doctrine in situations where it believed it would impede development of new technologies.[41]

But attached to the 2-1 appeals panel ruling on teletext, Judge Robert H. Bork, in an opinion joined by Judge Antonin Scalia, said the commission could take such a flexible approach because the fairness doctrine was not required by Congress. Instead, Bork said, the doctrine "derives from the mandate to serve the public interest."[42]

According to Bork, the fairness doctrine was not "a binding statutory obligation."[43] Rather, what Congress did in the 1959 amendment to Communications Act was to "ratify the [FCC's] longstanding position that the public interest standard authorizes the fairness doctrine."[44] But where did Bork draw from to come to this conclusion? Rather than use the more recent and thorough 1985 Fairness Report, he instead drew on an obscure line in the commission's 1983 teletext decision.[45] He totally ignored the commission's subsequent conclusions on the doctrine's statutory basis in its 1985 Fairness Doctrine Report.

The 1985 Report, of course, had concluded the fairness doctrine was probably unconstitutional because it violated the first amendment. But it also had concluded that the doctrine was a statutory requirement. Bork's finding in the *TRAC* case would provide just the ammunition Meredith and RTNDA were looking for in their appeals. "If the doctrine is not statutorily required, that would mean that the FCC was free to retain it or to eliminate it," said Timothy B. Dyk, the lawyer representing RTNDA in their appeal. And former FCC general counsel, Bruce E. Fein, whose language Bork drew on from the original FCC teletext decision, said providentially "It's clear fairness is gone. It's no longer going to be the rule for broadcasters."[46]

Andrew Jay Schwartzman of the Media Access Project, one of the organizations that challenged the FCC's action on the teletext issue, said the group would ask the full court to review the three-judge panel's ruling.[47] Schwartzman was joined by Henry Geller, a former FCC general counsel, and now director of the Washington Center for Public Policy Research. Geller said Bork's opinion was "wrong on the plain language of the statute, wrong on the legislative history [of the congressional amendment] and wrong on the case law."[48]

Mark Fowler's reaction, whose goal all along was to eliminate the doctrine, was more publicly subdued than his ex-general counsel Fein. Fowler said the Bork opinion was "very favorable from a First Amendment standpoint." And he said "the commission would cite Bork's opinion in the two cases (*RTNDA* and *Meredith*) involving the fairness doctrine to be argued before the court on September 30th."[49]

According to *Broadcasting*, the composition of the appeals panel hearing the arguments in the *RTNDA* and *Meredith* cases were "cause for cheer among broadcasters."[50] The panel consisted of Judges Laurence Silberman and Steven Williams, both new Reagan appointees, and U.S. senior District Judge William Jameson of Montana. Jameson had sat on several FCC cases, including those in which he helped affirm the commission in the radio deregulation and postcard renewal proceedings.

At the Tuesday, September 30 hearing, Judges Silberman and Williams of the U.S. Appeals Court, District of Columbia, questioned FCC general counsel Jack Smith. They asked Smith how the FCC could continue to enforce the fairness doctrine after issuing a policy statement declaring doctrine unconstitutional and having "chilling" affect on stations?[51] Their questions focussed on three issues, (1) the commission's 1985 Fairness Report; (2) the appeal by Meredith of the ruling that its station had violated the fairness doctrine in commercials promoting building of proposed nuclear power plant; and (3), the question of whether the Court had jurisdiction in either or both cases.[52]

As a result of recent ruling in *TRAC*, Silberman said, the Appeals Court no longer considered the fairness doctrine "a binding statutory obligation" on broadcast licensees. He continued, "From our point of view, the issue is resolved."[53] Smith, arguing for the commission, said the commission's Fairness Report deferred to Congress on the question of what action should be taken regarding the doctrine. And Smith said, Congress had made it clear that it expected the commission to continue to enforce the doctrine. "Congress has tied our hand," Smith said. When Judge Silberman asked Smith if the commission would follow instructions from the court, Smith said, "Of course, if the court reversed we wouldn't enforce the fairness doctrine."[54] What is interesting, is that Smith did not stress the commission's more recent 1985 conclusion of the doctrine's statutory basis. This analysis was more thorough, yet Smith chose not to stress it.

The first week of October, TRAC and MAP petitioned for an *en banc* rehearing of the *TRAC* decision. They contended that Bork's panel opinion "erroneously" upheld a position not even advanced by the commission. They did not challenge the entire panel decision, just the conclusion that the fairness doctrine was not written into the 1959 equal opportunities law. They based their appeal on the fact that the commission, a year after issuing its teletext decision, had concluded in 1985 it doubted it had the authority to repeal the doctrine.[55]

Bork's *TRAC* opinion got the immediate attention of Congress. Senator Hollings proposed adding language to the pending appropriations legislation, HR-5161, the second week of October. But broadcasters mobilized, and they were able to block the effort.[56] As a result of strong broadcast lobbying, the House-Senate Conference Committee rejected Senator Hollings' move. Instead, it approved the original Hollings' language instructing the FCC to look at alternative means of enforcing the fairness doctrine. The commission was to report to Congress on alternatives no later than September 30,1987, and during the interim, the agency was barred from taking any action on the doctrine.[57]

As indicated earlier, FCC commissioner James Quello had deep broadcast roots. By this time he, like the NAB, was moving away from strict marketplace rhetoric. In a speech before the Pennsylvania Association of Broadcasters, the second week of October, he suggested reviving a "raised-eyebrow campaign to tidy up broadcast journalism." He said "Top management and news directors must emphasize truth and responsibility in news and public affairs reporting over the individual quest for ratings, money and power."[58]

On Election Day, November 4, the Republicans lost eight seats in the Senate. This gave majority control in the Senate back to the Democrats for the first time since 1980. According to *Congressional Quarterly Weekly*, this would "set up a confrontation between a Democratic Congress and a Republican president who was still riding high in popularity polls."[59]

The original narrowly tailored intent of the fairness doctrine had by this time, long since been lost. Instead, it had turned into a political cause, and an ideologic cause. This can be seen by comparing two editorials which appeared in November. One, titled "The Fairness Doctrine is Shackling Broadcast," appeared in *Technology Review*. There the doctrine was described as "Orwellian." The editors claimed the fairness doctrine "does not seek to prevent government censorship. Rather, the overriding concern is to ensure that people are exposed to divergent viewpoints. While the First Amendment keeps the government out of the business of regulating speech, the effect of the Fairness Doctrine is to put the government squarely in that business."[60]

The second editorial, titled "Fowler's Obsession: Fighting the Fairness Doctrine," appeared in *The New Leader*. The editors cited that, "Last year, out of nearly 4,000 Fairness complaints against stations, only one was found valid. In 1984, there was again one adverse ruling against a broadcaster, this out of 6,800 complaints. In 1983, there were no actions against stations resulting from Fairness complaints."[61] *The New Leader* points out that these statistics are typical. With these kinds of numbers, it seems difficult to conclude the doctrine is "Orwellian." The editors of *The New Leader* viewed the fairness doctrine as a "nominal, sometimes token presentation of opposing viewpoints was enough to satisfy the regulation.[62]

The U.S. Circuit Court of Appeals, District of Columbia, Tuesday, December 16, refused MAP's and TRAC's request for a full-court rehearing of the *TRAC* decision.[63] They fell one vote short of the majority approval needed to gain a full-court rehearing. Two of the court's 11 judges did not participate in the ruling. So even though the decision was 5 to 4 in favor of a rehearing, it was one vote short of a majority. Judges Abner J. Mikva, Harry T. Edwards, Spottswood W. Robinson III, Kenneth W. Starr and Ruth Bader Ginsburg voted to rehear the case. Judges Laurence H. Silberman, James L. Buckley, Stephen L. Williams and Robert Bork voted against the rehearing.[64] Chief Judge Patricia M. Wald and Judge Douglas H. Ginsburg did not participate. Justice Antonin Scalia had been elevated to the Supreme Court after the decision was reached.

The division within the court was reflected in the statements accompanying the court's order. Judge Abner Mikva wrote a dissent, in which Judge Harry T. Edward joined. Mikva's dissent declared the panel's conclusion was "flatly wrong."[65] Bork also issued an opinion defending the earlier panel ruling.[66]

Judge Abner Mikva's dissenting opinion said the panel decision, holding that the fairness doctrine was not a "binding statutory obligation" under the Communications Act of 1934 ... is flatly wrong." Mikva said "In amending the act in 1959, congress not only recognized and preserved an administrative construction, it explicitly approved of, ratified and codified the fairness doctrine."[67]

He continued, "Indeed, the legislative history again evinces a recognition that the fairness principle is embodied in the act itself." Mikva pointed out that "This court has repeatedly considered the fairness doctrine as part of the statutory framework of the act. As Judge Robinson explained for the court, "[the] language placed in Section 315(1) in 1959 ... codifies the fairness doctrine formulated by the commission in 1949. The doctrine ... has ... received explicit statutory recognition, in the 1959 amendment."[68]

The conclusion reached in the commission's 1985 Fairness Report was not lost on Mikva. As he said:

> Significantly, after thoroughly canvassing the act and its history, the commission recently declined to conclude that "it had the authority without further congressional action to eliminate the fairness doctrine." In responding to the petition for review in this

case, the commission never argued that the fairness doctrine was *not* statutorily mandated. That argument is a construct of the majority of the panel who heard the case.[69]

Mikva concluded his dissent saying, "By the 1959 amendment the commission is not simply authorized to impose the fairness doctrine, it is compelled to do so. The doctrine has been encapsulated by Section 315 of the act, and the courts overreach to undo it."[70]

But Bork's opinion carried the day. Bork's argument was that "It is plain, therefore, that in the 1959 amendment Congress was disclaiming any intent to dismantle the commission's fairness policy."[71] His interpretation was that:

> There is every indication that Congress ratified the commission's authority to evolve the fairness doctrine under the act's public interest standard. But there is also every indication that Congress went no further. It did not legislate that, having created the fairness doctrine, the commission was henceforward required to keep it and apply it as it stood in 1959.
>
> The dissent is quite correct in saying that "[t]he primacy of congress as policy-maker should not be blunted or eviscerated by courts which find either the policy or the policy-makers in *error*." That is precisely the reason we should not impute to Congress a statute that it never debated or enacted.[72]

As the Appeals Court was deciding not to review its *TRAC* decision, Fowler was denying that the agency had "taken a dive" on the fairness doctrine in court. Fowler's response to this claim came in reply to a series of questions that Representative Swift had submitted to the agency as follow-up to an October hearing. There, Swift said he believed the agency did not properly defend its own policies in several recent cases (*TRAC*, *Meredith*, and *RTNDA*).[73] But Fowler defended the commission, saying the FCC was compelled to disclose to the court its differences with Congress on the doctrine. According to Fowler, the agency had no alternative.[74]

In October, Swift had accused the commission of intentionally making weak cases in court for policies with which it disagreed. But Fowler defended the commission's actions by saying the commission general counsel "has responsibility to keep the Court advised of pertinent developments related to ... litigation." Fowler's December follow-up response appeared to admit that he had been wrong in denying in October that the commission purposely had raised doubts about agency rules in court. Now in December, Fowler claimed that he had not known details of the agency's brief to court. The commission brief had raised constitutional questions about the equal time rule as part of the commission defense.[75]

The last two months of 1986 changed the outlook for the 100th Congress. Democrats hoped Reagan would be on the defensive for the first time since his 1980 election. The Democratic victory in the Senate brought in Ernest Hollings (D-South Carolina) as chairman of the Senate Commerce Committee. In the House, John Dingell (D-Michigan) remained chair of the Energy and Commerce Committee. And it appeared Edward J. Markey (D-Massachusetts), whose views were similar to his predecessor, Tim Wirth(D-Colorado), would chair the House Telecommunications Subcommittee.[76]

January to August 1987

Mark Fowler announced his intention to resign as chairman, in January 1987. Dennis Patrick was designated as his replacement. Whether Patrick accelerated the dismissal of the doctrine is conjecture, but he obviously felt no duty to maintain it.

In February the *Meredith* and *RTNDA* cases were remanded by the Court back to the commission. Though the commission had obviously hoped the Appeals Court would rule the fairness doctrine unconstitutional, it did not oblige the commission. But with the record the commission had developed in the preceding six years, it was finally in a position to move on the doctrine itself.

Congress, in 1987, also finally was able to muster enough support to pass a bill codifying the doctrine. But it could not muster enough support to overcome Reagan's veto of it. And finally, in August, with decreased credibility in the Court, and increasing anger which would turn to rage in Congress, the commission itself dismissed the fairness doctrine. As a result of this action, Congress would involve itself even further into the daily functioning of the agency. It even refused to confirm any new commissioners for almost two full years. This forced the commission to operate with only a quorum-minimum of three commissioners.

On Tuesday, January 6, the 100th Congress reconvened. Both the House and the Senate were back in Democratic control for the first time since 1980. Senator Ernest Hollings of South Carolina assumed the chair of the Commerce Committee, and Daniel K. Inouye of Hawaii headed the Communications Subcommittee. Hollings had served as chairman of the Communications Subcommittee in the late 1970's. He was a 20-year veteran of the Senate. Hollings was not only chairman of the Commerce Committee, he was also chairman of the Appropriations Subcommittee which had jurisdiction over the agency's budget.[77]

Inouye's views were similar to Hollings'. He was known as a masterful politician and an inside player. John Dingell (D-Michigan) retained control of the House Energy and Commerce Committee. And the new chairman of the House Telecommunications Subcommittee would be Massachusetts Democrat Edward J. Markey.

FCC chairman Mark Fowler, who was renominated by Reagan on June 5, 1986, still had not received a confirmation hearing. Some believed the Democratic takeover of the Senate reduced his chances of being confirmed.[78] Democratic dissent had always been there, but without a majority in both Houses, it was diffused. But now the Democrats controlled the majority in both Houses.

On Thursday, January 15, House Energy and Commerce Committee Chairman John Dingell, speaking at a Federal Communications Bar Association luncheon in Washington, called for a return to the public trustee concept in broadcasting. Dingell blamed the FCC for creating an environment hostile to the public interest standard.[79] He criticized the commission's application of marketplace ideology to broadcasters, and indicated he would not tolerate wholesale deregulation. The Communications Act, he said, "does not treat broadcasters as owners of the airwaves that they use." He called FCC marketplace ideology "misguided" for relying "entirely on unrestricted private advantage to protect the public interest."[80]

Dingell did say, though, he was "heartened ... that the National Association of Broadcasters has issued a position paper recognizing that broadcasters do indeed have public interest responsibilities and rejecting the marketplace approach to broadcast regulation."[81]

On Monday, January 5, 1987, Senator Proxmire (D-Wisconsin) again reintroduced his First Amendment Clarification Act. Proxmire's legislation would repeal the commission's authority to impose the fairness doctrine, the measure also would repeal the equal time rule, and program objectivity standards for public broadcasters.[82] Proxmire's bill would never be reported out of committee.

After almost six years as chairman of the FCC, Fowler, in a letter to the White House, January 16, said he felt it was time to end his stewardship. Fowler's resignation letter ended with a plea for "full" first amendment rights for broadcasters.[83]

The speculation was that Reagan would name Dennis Patrick to succeed Fowler. Fowler was expected to remain as chairman until after the NAB convention, March 28-31.[84] Though Patrick was considered the favorite for Fowler's position, Mimi Dawson also waged a lobbying campaign for the post.[85] Dawson's candidacy was championed chiefly by her former boss, Senator Robert Packwood (R-Oregon). But Packwood, who had numerous difficulties with the Reagan White House, by now had lost his political clout. A number of recent actions at the commission, such as Patrick staff member Diana Killory's move to FCC general counsel, lent credence to the speculation favoring Patrick.[86] Also, Bradley Holmes, another former Patrick adviser, was now chief of the Mass Media bureau's Policy and Rules division. And Kathie Levitz, yet another former Patrick aide, was made an attorney with the Office of Plans and Policy.[87] Possibly the most significant reason only Dawson and Patrick were considered top contenders for the chairmanship was that, as sitting commissioners, they could assume the chairmanship without Senate confirmation.[88]

The timing of Fowler's resignation itself was the subject of speculation. *Broadcasting* reported that many believed Fowler wanted to "avoid the rancorous Senate confirmation hearing that had been promised by Democrats."[89]

Tuesday, January 16, the U.S. Appeals Court, District of Columbia, issued its decision in the cases brought by RTNDA and Meredith.[90] The commission had hoped it would rule the fairness doctrine unconstitutional. But instead the Appeals Court panel said RTNDA's request for consideration of constitutionality question, based on the FCC's 1985 Fairness Report, was in the wrong court. The Appeals Court panel said RTNDA's appeal belonged in the U.S. District Court.[91]

In *Meredith*, the court panel chastised the FCC. Saying the commissioners had taken an oath to defend the constitution, and for the commission to enforce an FCC-generated policy that it thought unconstitutional, could constitute a violation of the commissioners' oath. With this statement, the court remanded *Meredith* back to the commission. The Appeals panel told the commission it must discharge its constitutional obligations by explicitly considering Meredith's claim that enforcement of the fairness doctrine against Meredith deprived it of its constitutional rights. "The Commission's failure to do so seems to us the very paradigm of arbitrary and capricious administrative action."[92] Though exposing the impropriety of the commission's behavior, this language was to provide the legal justification for the agency's later action dismissing the doctrine.

The court also said: "Of course, the Commission need not confront that issue [constitutionality] if it concludes that in light of its fairness report it may not or should not enforce the doctrine because it is contrary to the public interest."[93] As noted in *Television Digest*, the court set no timetable for that consideration.[94]

But the commission wasted little time. On Friday, January 23, it released an Inquiry on the fairness doctrine.[95] In announcing its Inquiry, the commission said it was reopening the fairness proceeding to consider the policy and constitutional issues raised, and, in light of the "general importance of the issues in the particular case," it invited comments from "interested members of the public as well as from the parties in the particular adjudication."[96]

Even though the court said the commission did not have to rule on the doctrine's constitutionality, the commission's Inquiry sought to do just that. It sought public comment on whether, in light of its 1985 Fairness Report, enforcement of the fairness doctrine was constitutional or contrary to the public interest.[97]

When interviewed by *Television Digest*, Fowler was asked if he was seeking the doctrine's elimination immediately. He avoided answering the question directly. He said, instead, "Where you have freedoms which are at the core of the First Amendment... the law teaches us that any restrictions in this area need to be looked at constantly and promptly evaluated. Generally, that argues for moving with some dispatch, particularly since we had the omnibus inquiry on this in 1985."[98]

The Inquiry was approved unanimously by the commissioners. Comments were due by February 25th. Commissioner Quello, in a separate statement, said he "steadfastly" believed Congress codified doctrine in the 1959 amendments to Communications Act. He said his preference would be to delay until the Supreme Court ruled on the *TRAC* case because questions of the statutory basis of the doctrine "are central" to the FCC's ability to eliminate or enforce it.[99]

On Thursday, February 5, President Reagan announced his intention to designate Dennis R. Patrick as FCC chairman.[100] Patrick would assume the chair effective upon the departure of Fowler. Reagan formally notified Congress on Wednesday, February 4, of his decision to designate Dennis Patrick as chairman. But Reagan made no announcement of his choice of a new commissioner to replace Fowler on the 5-member commission. Patrick, in a released statement, said he was "deeply honored... I share the view of many that Mark Fowler has been, and continues to be, an outstanding chairman."[101]

Commissioner Quello said he hoped Patrick would be "a little more sensitive" to Congress than Fowler.[102] *Broadcasting* said of Patrick, that "Those hoping for a more compromising spirit may be in for an unpleasant surprise." It cited sources as saying that Patrick, if anything, may be more conservative and "more ideological" than Fowler.[103]

Fowler had the advantage of a Republican controlled Senate, even though Democrats controlled the House. But Patrick faced a Senate and House controlled by Democrats. There was also much less enthusiasm for deregulation than there was in 1981. Congress seemed hopeful of Patrick, though. It believed Patrick had indicated he would leave changing the fairness doctrine to Congress, rather than acting unilaterally.[104] Patrick announced he would decline interviews until after he was sworn in as chairman.

With Fowler's announced resignation, came the usual flurry of activity, and speculation of naming a replacement. *Television Digest* said on February 16, at least six candidates were "viable or somewhat viable."[105] And by the end of the month, Peter Pitsch, chief of the FCC's Office of Plans and Policy, was said to be a leading candidate. But citing an unnamed White House official, *Broadcasting* reported Pitsch, who was said to be Patrick's candidate, would "probably not get the appointment."[106] Allen Moore, minority chief of staff for Senate Commerce Committee, and Craig Smith, president of the Freedom of Expression Foundation, were two other of at least 10 candidates named as possible appointments by February 23.

Representative Markey (D-Massachusetts), new chairman of the House Telecommunications Subcommittee, spoke at a conference sponsored by *Communications Daily*, and the Washington law firm Wilkes, Artis, Hedrick & Lane, the first week in February. Markey said "The time has come to legislate in favor of the fairness doctrine." He said the FCC's decision to start an inquiry into the doctrine's constitutionality "flouts the express desire of Congress that the FCC not modify or repeal the fairness doctrine."[107]

Markey said it was "time to resurrect the FCC as a regulatory agency, not an agency which dispassionately watches an unbridled marketplace work its will, while turning a blind eye to the interest of the consumer."[108] He charged that chairman Fowler had "taken the position that... [the] Communications Act of 1934 is an annoyance which must be circumvented." Markey said he believed "we can redirect the Commission toward its original and vital mission--to protect the public interest."[109]

Markey announced that the House Telecommunications Subcommittee would hold a hearing on March 18, on the fairness doctrine. All five FCC commissioners would be invited as witnesses. Markey said he wanted the hearing to "ensure that Congress has an opportunity to present its viewpoints on any attempt to gut or codify the doctrine."[110]

Senator Hollings also told an NAB state leadership conference in Washington, the last week in February, that legislation to codify the fairness doctrine into law would be introduced in the Senate shortly.[111]

Friday, February 13, the FCC finally issued a Notice launching the separate inquiry mandated by Congress. The inquiry would look at alternative enforcement mechanisms to the fairness doctrine.[112] The Notice did not stipulate possible alternatives, but instead invited comments on: (1) Abandoning existing case-by-case complaints enforcement in favor of reviews during license renewals; (2) Imposing a test moratorium on enforcement; (3) Marketwide enforcement; (4) Replacing the doctrine with a so-called "access time" requirement. The Notice specified comments were due in 45 days, and replies 30 days later on May 13.[113]

Television Digest said, "As expected, tensions were high at the Wednesday, February 18, FCC oversight hearing. It reported Congressional leaders were angry that Fowler had been quoted as saying he wanted the fairness doctrine eliminated before he left the commission in the spring. *Television Digest* reported that congressmen were also angry the commission was moving slowly on the congressional requirement for evaluation of alternative enforcement mechanisms to fairness doctrine. Hollings criticized the commission for waiting some four months to issue the congressionally mandated inquiry.[114] Hollings also said he thought the proceeding should have been started before the commission began its related inquiry involving the *Meredith* case, which was probing the constitutionality of the doctrine. Fowler, in what was to prove a deceptive maneuver, announced that a decision in *Meredith* case would not be made by the commissioners until the agency had completed its report to Congress on alternatives.[115] The alternative report had a September 30, 1987, deadline.

The comments received by the February 25, deadline for the agency's reopened inquiry into the fairness doctrine, contained no surprises. Most broadcasters urged the FCC to dismiss the doctrine. In joint comments, the RTNDA, CBS, NAB, the Freedom of Expression Foundation, Gannett Co., Meredith Corp., Multimedia Inc., Post-Newsweek Stations Inc., and the Society of Professional Journalists, Sigma Delta Chi, said they believed that the FCC lacked authority to continue enforcing the doctrine. "We hereby request that the commission take action to eliminate the fairness doctrine on the grounds that it is unconstitutional and contrary to the public interest," they said.[116]

The commission, February 27, asked the U.S. Appeals Court, District of Columbia, to reconsider its January decision that the *RTNDA* appeal belonged in District Court. FCC general counsel Smith argued this conclusion was "flatly inconsistent with the statutory scheme for judicial review of FCC actions."[117] At the same time, RTNDA also asked the Appeals Court to rehear the case. And, in a separate filing, the FCC asked the Appeals Court to hold in abeyance a final ruling in *RTNDA* until the commission acted in the *Meredith* appeal.

Legislation to codify the fairness doctrine was introduced in the Senate on Thursday, March 12, by Senators Hollings, Inouye, and Danforth.[118] The bill, S-742, received prompt action. The bill itself was short. It said that the spectrum remains a scarce resource and that competition and diversity of ideas can not be measured merely by how many alternative kinds of services may be offered in the marketplace.

The spectrum was a public resource, and broadcasters use was contingent upon the industry's assuming a trustee role. *Television Digest* reported that Senator Proxmire (D-Wisconsin), author of a countermeasure to scrap the fairness doctrine, S-22, threatened a filibuster with Senator Packwood (R-Oregon).[119]

The Communications Subcommittee held a hearing on S-742 on Wednesday, March 18. Among the witnesses were: FCC chairman Fowler; Charles Ferris, former FCC chairman now with an Washington law firm; Robert Shayon, Professor at the University of Pennsylvania, Annenberg School; John Spain, news director, WBRZ Baton Rouge and immediate past president of RTNDA; Craig Smith, president of the Freedom of Expression Foundation (and FCC candidate); Thomas Elkins, president-general manager, KNUI (AM) Kahului, Hawaii; and Ray Mosher, dean emeritus of University of Missouri School of Journalism.[120]

Little new information was provided at the hearing, and not surprisingly, Fowler said that the agency had documented "the absolute unfairness of letting federal regulators 'correct' and 'improve' viewpoints with which they disagree.[121] Tuesday, March 24, on a 14-4 vote, the Senate Commerce Committee sent the fairness doctrine bill (S-742) to the floor for final action.

The committee action came after a brief mark-up at which most senators expressed unqualified support for the bill to codify the fairness doctrine. But Packwood and Stevens promised countermeasures and floor fights. Packwood had reintroduced his bill,[122] S-827, March 24. It was identical to last year's S-1038. It would repeal relevant Sections 312(1) and 315, and added to Section 325 of Communications Act.[123] Like Proxmire's bill, it would never be reported out of committee.

The RTNDA, and the FCC, were given another opportunity to persuade the U.S. Court of Appeals, District of Columbia, that it had jurisdiction over the constitutional issue involved in RTNDA's appeal. The Appeals Court, the third week of March, granted a rehearing in the case. It ordered the RTNDA and the commission to file briefs in three weeks.[124]

Television Digest reported March 30, that Bradley Holmes, chief of Mass Media Bureau Policy Division was emerging as the front-runner for the FCC commissioner vacancy. *Television Digest* reported

Holmes had the strong support of chairman-designate, commissioner Patrick.[125]

Tuesday, March 31, 1987, Mark Fowler delivered his final speech, as FCC chairman, to the NAB convention in Dallas.[126]   Fowler first reviewed the conditions existing when he began is term.   He said, "You, the broadcaster, had suffered under years of error by trial regulation."   He contended, "The FCC tried to pretend you were second class citizens about your first amendment rights."   He then reviewed what he considered to be the reasons for his managerial success. The most important, he said, was:

> The first is a mathematical rule that really applies if you plan to be Chairman. Rule one states: Divide by two, add one and round off. What I'm referring to is getting a majority vote through the Commission.

Fowler said his second managerial principle was, "Whatever can be leaked, will be leaked." He said Washington was less like a sewer than a sieve when it comes to information getting out prematurely.

His third principle of success was, "Park your car in the same spot every day." He said by this he meant, "If you have a principled way of looking at the world, and you stick to it, you can go about doing your job with sincerity and conviction."

His fourth, and final, principle was "Remember that you're not a lobster." He said this meant, "you were given a backbone. Don't be afraid to honor it by using it."

He used this final principle as one last attempt to rally broadcasters to get "radio and television on the right side of the first amendment line." He said broadcasters had the "leadership right here in this room. Use it. You've got the political clout. Wield it."

Also speaking at the NAB convention was FCC Mass Media Bureau Chief ,James McKinney.   In a similar vein to Fowler, McKinney said, the agency would "continue to work very hard" to do away with attempts to regulate programming," and would continue to "press for abolishing the fairness doctrine."   McKinney told broadcasters that the fairness doctrine "chills your speech... without a doubt."[127]

In a final interview with the *Washington Post*, Sunday, April 19, Fowler said he wished he "would have closed the doors of the FCC for good" when he walked out of the building for the last time as the agency's chairman.[128] Fowler said he was disappointed by his inability to get the fairness doctrine repealed. "I think it is unconstitutional and bad policy," he said.[129]

Also leaving with Fowler was Albert Halprin. Halprin had been Fowler's chief architect of telephone deregulation. Fowler and Halprin would eventually go into practice together.

Dennis Roy Patrick officially took over as chairman on Saturday, April 18. Patrick may have shared some of Fowler's libertarian views, but he did not seem to take them quite to the extreme. For example, in a unanimous decision the third week of April, and Fowler's last official meeting, the commission said it would regulate indecent broadcasts and set forth standards it would use.[130] This signalled the first movement by the commission back into content regulation.

But Patrick, as indicated earlier, faced different conditions from that of his predecessor. First, Fowler had six years as the head of the agency during the ascendancy of the Reagan administration. Patrick could not count on much more than two years, the remainder of Reagan's term. While Fowler had a Republican Senate to run some interference for him, Patrick was confronted by both houses of Congress dominated by the Democrats. Also Fowler had a subtle edge Patrick would not have, Fowler had two commissioners, Patrick and Mimi Dawson, competing to succeed him. Some speculated they may have been more manageable because they wanted to be perceived as part of the same team. And finally, the broadcast industry appeared to be firmly behind Fowler. *Broadcasting* said Fowler's experience in the broadcasting business helped him considerably.[131]

Patrick would have a short honeymoon with Congress. He had offered to meet one-on-one with all the members of the agency's congressional oversight subcommittees.[132] *Broadcasting* reported that this seemed to please Congressional leaders.

But Patrick also gave some indication of what to expect in his first public interview as chairman. He told *Broadcasting* that what he was loyal to were his principles. He said, "One of the ideas with respect to which I might be called an ideologue is that we should be suspicious of the proposition that government can most effectively solve the problem, and we should rely where we can on marketplace mechanisms." He continued, "The second idea in which I believe is the fundamental wisdom of the First Amendment."[133]

Patrick immediately announced several major appointments: (1) Peter Pitsch, currently chief of Office of Plans and Policy (OPP), who had made a run for vacant FCC seat, as his chief of staff. John Haring, currently an OPP staffer, would succeed Pitsch, jumping over deputy chief Thomas Spavins. Gerald Brock, chief of Accounting and Audits Division of Common Carrier Bureau, was named Bureau Chief, succeeding Albert Halprin. Remaining in their posts for the near term were James McKinney, Mass Media Bureau chief; John Kamp, chief of Office of Congressional and Public Affairs; Edward Minkel, managing director. And Patrick brought the following aides from his office: Engineer Lex Felker, ex-OPP; James Schlichting, ex-Common Carrier.[134]

The first congressional test for Patrick came Tuesday, April 21. He appeared before the Senate Communications Subcommittee in an FCC oversight hearing. *Television Digest* citing unnamed Hill sources, said there was nearly unanimous agreement in predicting eased FCC-Congress tensions. These sources said this was primarily because of "differences in style between Patrick and Fowler, even though their philosophies are very similar."[135] This prediction, of course, failed to materialize.

Chairman Patrick told the Senate Communications Subcommittee that "broadcast and cable matters will be among top priorities for the FCC."[136] He emphasized consumer and public interest angles on issues. *Television Digest* reported this struck a conciliatory note for many on the committee. Patrick also sought to diffuse tensions with Congress on FCC oversight. He said, "The Congress quite properly takes the lead role." Stressing he understood the agency was accountable to Congress, he said "The FCC is a creature of Congress and I understand Congress can by statute overturn anything done by the Commission."[137]

Television Digest, April 20, citing an unnamed GOP source, said that the appointment of the fifth commissioner "reportedly has been put on hold by the White House and no action is expected for several weeks because of 'other sensitive political appointments' pending." This meant Patrick could operate with four-person FCC for several months. *Television Digest* said it had been told that all 13 Republican senators who had voted to override President Reagan's veto on a highway bill had been put on "black list" at the White House. And "their pet projects and desired appointments were on hold."[138]

Tuesday, April 21, the Senate approved S-742. S-742 barred the FCC from scrapping the fairness doctrine. Over objections from the

Reagan administration, the Senate voted 59 to 31 to write the doctrine into permanent law. The Senate's action was supported by most Democrats and opposed by a majority of Republicans. But Senator John C. Danforth (R-Missouri), had been a co-sponsor of the bill.[139] The same legislation had been introduced as a House bill[140] (HR-1934), April 2.

Television Digest reported that Reagan's cabinet-level Domestic Policy Council was considering asking President Reagan to veto the bill (S-742). *Television Digest* reported that fueling the veto talk was a Justice Department opinion, released April 21, that opposed the bill. But the Justice opinion did not do its own constitutional analysis. Instead, it relied on the FCC's. The Justice Department said it was impressed by the FCC arguments, and said the doctrine appeared unconstitutional. It said, of the commission's 1985 Fairness Report, "We have seldom seen a more impressive or facially plausible analysis of this kind of difficult, fact-based, constitutional issue. Unless there exists a more powerful counter-analysis that we are not aware of, the FCC report in our view satisfactorily demonstrates that the fairness doctrine is now unconstitutional."[141]

In a May 4, 1987, interview with *Television Digest*, Patrick disputed that he was "aloof," an "ideologue," or "a friend of Hollywood."[142] He also said he did not use the term "public trustee" in describing broadcasters' obligations to the public. He said this was because:

> [T]hat term carries with it a number of implications about regulation, past and present... I believe that anybody who controls a medium of mass communications in a democracy has public interest responsibilities... The real issue is who defines what those responsibilities are and who ensures that they are going to be executed. And it is with respect to those second set of issues that I believe we should rely more so on the marketplace and less so on the government.[143]

In the interview, Patrick said that even if Congress passes legislation codifying the fairness doctrine, "it would not it seems to me necessarily resolve the constitutional question. Eventually the courts will have to resolve that."[144] Patrick also said he planned to continue Fowler's policy of holding commission meetings only once a month. Also, most items would continue to be acted on by circulation, with public and interested parties receiving no advance notice.[145] This was one mechanism developed by the commission in an attempt to diffuse some of the micromanagement of Congress.

Dennis Patrick's first meeting as chairman was Thursday, May 14. *Broadcasting* described it as a "not-terribly-taxing agenda."[146] There Patrick released printed remarks listing the FCC's objectives under his leadership. His remarks said:

> The focus during my chairmanship will be on maximizing the public interest benefits to be derived from our communications resources. While I firmly believe the public has benefitted from the deregulatory path the commission has pursued, we should never confuse the end with the means. Deregulation is not an end in itself, but has validity only insofar as it serves the public interest.[147]

His six commission objectives, under his chairmanship, were:

> (1)   Promote, wherever possible, a competitive marketplace for the development and use of communications facilities and services;
> (2)   Provide a regulatory framework which permits markets for communications services to function effectively, while eliminating regulations which are unnecessary or inimical to the public interest;
> (3)   Promote efficiency in the allocation, licensing and use of the electromagnetic spectrum;
> (4)   Protect and promote the interests of the American public in international communications;
> (5)   Provide service to the public in the most efficient, expeditious manner possible; and
> (6)   Eliminate government action which infringes upon freedom of speech and the press."[148]

Ignoring a veto threat by the White House, the House Telecommunications Subcommittee, Thursday, May 7, reported favorably, HR-1934, to codify fairness doctrine into law. The measure next went to the parent House Energy and Commerce Committee. By a vote of 33-8, on Wednesday, May 13, the full Energy and Commerce Committee approved the legislation. HR-1934 was expected to get to the House floor sometime in June.[149] *Television Digest* quoted a letter from the White House to the NAB, that said, the "White House declined to say definitely whether the President would veto the measure.[150]

The function. and the public visibility, of the FCC's general counsel had increased markedly during the Fowler years. This public visibility began with Fowler's first general counsel, Stephen Sharp. It peaked with Bruce Fein. Jack Smith, Fein's successor, tried to take some of the public visibility out of the position by trying to disassociate the General Counsel Office from the policy role Fein had savored. This was easier said than done, though. What then could be expected of the newly named FCC general counsel, Diana Killory? By way of background, she had graduated cum laude from Harvard Law School in 1979. After graduating she came to Washington to work for the law firm of Steptoe & Johnson. After nearly four years there, she was recruited by Bruce Fein, then the general counsel at the FCC. She began at the FCC in May, 1983, as special counsel for legal policy in Fein's office.[151]

When Patrick arrived at the commission in 1983 he asked for recommendations for a legal assistant and Killory was recommended.[152] She became his assistant, and was named his senior advisor soon afterwards. In her role as senior advisor, she worked closely with Patrick on developing his positions. She also helped him write speeches, and accompanied him to trade shows and other functions. She had switched from being a registered Democrat to registered independent. In 1986 she became a registered Republican.[153]

The House on Wednesday, June 3, easily enacted HR-1974, codifying the fairness doctrine. The House passed the legislation by a vote of 302-102. *Congressional Quarterly Weekly* reported that although the Reagan administration had urged lawmakers to vote against the bill, Reagan had still not said whether he would veto it.[154]

James McKinney, FCC Mass Media Chief since 1983, and a veteran of 24 years with the commission, was appointed Tuesday, June 16, to be deputy assistant to the President and director of White House Military Office. McKinney would handle telecommunications matters, and would report to Rhett Dawson, husband of commissioner Dawson.[155] Patrick immediately appointed Deputy Chief, William Johnson, as acting chief of Mass Media Bureau. Initial speculation was that Patrick would appoint his former aide, Bradley Holmes, currently chief of Bureau's Policy and Rules Division, as permanent chief.[156]

The marketplace approach, which characterized the Fowler commission, was now slowly eroding. For example, James Quello, in a speech at the Broadcast Promotion and Marketing Executives meeting in Atlanta, the second week of June, said broadcast deregulation had "gone too far in the last couple of years," under Mark Fowler's chairmanship.[157] Quello said that the FCC, and its new chairman Dennis Patrick, would cause the pendulum to swing back from a laissez-faire, let-the-marketplace-decide philosophy to one of aggressive reinstituting of new regulation.[158] But this did not mean he had changed his mind with respect to the fairness doctrine. As he said, "The commission should not get involved in dictating program content." He concluded his remarks saying "I still think the phrase 'public interest, convenience and [sic] necessity' means something."[159]

The U.S. Supreme Court, the second week of June, refused without comment to accept an appeal of the 1986 FCC action denying the application of the fairness doctrine to teletext transmissions.[160] This was the appeal made by TRAC and MAP. Because of optimism generated by congressional passage of fairness codification, MAP's Andrew Schwartzman mistakenly said that the groups were not disappointed because, "what we lost in court we're getting back from Congress."[161]

The House Telecommunications Subcommittee held an FCC oversight hearing the second week of June. Though some claimed Patrick was on a honeymoon with Congress, it was a strained honeymoon at best. Representative John Dingell opened the hearing by asking Patrick, "Does the commission have any intention of enforcing or defining the fairness doctrine in a fashion that in fact nullifies or weakens the doctrine?" Patrick replied, "If the fairness doctrine is codified by the Congress and its constitutionality is sustained, we will enforce it in good faith and to the letter of the law."[162]

And when Dingell asked Patrick, "If the question of the fairness doctrine constitutionality arises in court, will the commission defend it, will the commission attack it or will the commission sit back and let matters take their course?" Patrick replied evasively, "Mr. Chairman, that is a question I would want to discuss with my general counsel." Patrick continued, though, "The commission's position with regard to the constitutionality of the fairness doctrine was set forth in our fairness report, wherein we concluded that the constitutionality of the doctrine was at least suspect in light of the multiplicity of broadcasting sources in the marketplace today."[163]

Representative Swift, noticing a loophole in Patrick's answers to Dingell's question, asked: "I did notice that in an answer to the chairman of the full committee with regard to the fairness doctrine, you said that if it passed and is constitutional you would enforce it. Did you mean that you would enforce it if it's passed only after there has been litigation demonstrating its constitutionality, or will you presume its constitutionality until it's otherwise ruled?" Patrick replied, "Well, sir, if Congress passes the fairness doctrine, I assume that we'll assume that it's the law and we'll enforce the law unless it's held to be unconstitutional."[164]

With congressional passage of the fairness doctrine bill, the question now became whether Reagan would veto the measure. Both Justice and Commerce Departments recommended a veto. And Senator Bob Packwood, a leading opponent to the bill in the Senate, was quoted as saying he felt he could command the votes necessary to sustain a veto.[165]

Wednesday, June 10, the *Washington Post* ran an editorial titled, "'Fairness' Calls for a Veto." The editorial opened saying, "Ignoring the fact that there is nothing 'fair' about the so-called 'fairness doctrine' with which government can control the broadcasting of ideas in this country, Congress has voted to convert this chilling federal regulation into a full-blown law."[166] The editorial concluded by saying, "Our view does come from an organization with a direct interest in broadcasting, but it stems from a belief that the 'fairness doctrine' undermines independent, sound journalism by inserting governmental dictates. That's dangerous, unhelpful and deceptive. The measure should not become law."[167]

Television Digest reported on June 15, that the White House staff had recommended that Reagan veto the bill on "policy and constitutional grounds." The move by the White House advisers had been recommended by both the Justice and Commerce Departments, NTIA, and OMB.[168] The bill was sent to the White House, June 8. And on Tuesday, June 19, 1987, Reagan vetoed the bill. In his message returning the bill to the Senate, he said, "This type of content-based regulation by the Federal Government is, in my judgment, antagonistic to the freedom of expression guaranteed by the First Amendment."[169] Reagan concluded his veto message saying:

> S. 742 simply cannot be reconciled with the freedom of speech and the press secured by our Constitution. It is, in my judgment, unconstitutional. Well-intentioned as S. 742 may be, it would be inconsistent with the First Amendment and with the American tradition of independent journalism. Accordingly, I am compelled to disapprove this measure.[170]

Reagan knew he needed broadcaster support to protect against an over-ride, and he got his message out to them through his staff. For example, White House Chief of Staff Howard Baker, speaking at the annual conference of the Radio and Television News Directors Association in Washington on Friday, June 26, said:

> We are hearing rumblings, as you are, that the bill to codify the Fairness Doctrine is not dead but merely dozing, and that it will be revived in the fullness of time and attached to some other piece of legislation which is veto-proof. My friends, I am here to advise you, and the Congress, too, if it cares to listen in, that in his present frame of mind, the President of the United States considers no legislation veto-proof.[171]

Baker's remarks need to be understood in context. Voting largely along party lines, 53-45, on June 23, the Senate had already agreed to refer Reagan's veto message to the Commerce Committee. *Congressional Quarterly Weekly* reported that Committee Democrats said they planed to attach the fairness doctrine to other legislation the White House may find more difficult to resist. The Democrats also acknowledged they lacked the two-thirds majority needed to override the President.[172] And this was how the *Washington Post*, on Tuesday, June 23, described the Commerce Committee's action: "The Senate gave President Reagan his first veto victory of the year yesterday as it ducked a showdown vote on ... the fairness doctrine."[173] It went on to say that Reagan had vetoed only three measures this year, and Congress overrode the first two: clean-water legislation and a bill to reauthorize highway and mass transit programs. And, as the *Post* put it, "the fairness doctrine did not have the same lure as money for water-cleanup and highway-building efforts."[174]

Between 1984 and 1986, the FCC received 19,565 fairness doctrine complaints. Of these 19,565 complaints, it pursued only 18 of them with the station involved. And of these 18, it had ruled that there was a violation in just one case, Meredith Broadcasting.[175]   To the Democratic leadership in Congress this was a symptom; the disease was the commission itself. Congress' remedy: micromanagement. As Swift put it, in a *Television Digest* interview:

> What we should be doing is making policy, not micromanaging. "What they [FCC] should be doing is following our policy. Unfortunately, when an agency refuses to follow the policy, they invite micromanagement. The FCC has been sending out engraved invitations for micromanagement for six years now.[176]

Senator Hollings and Representative Ed Markey, also, readily admitted that it was their intention to exercise even greater control over the FCC and its policies. Hollings said what Congress was doing was "common sense," returning "to correct what has gone wrong" with deregulation.[177]

Interviewed for the same article in *Television Digest*, Patrick said, that as much as he admired Fowler, and the work he did, "I think that eventually the Congress will view me in my own light and judge me and this commission in what we do and the way in which we approach issues."[178]   One cannot help but wonder what kind of loaded statement that was.

As for increased Congressional micromanagement, Patrick said, he felt that as long as Congress had empowered an agency to perform certain congressional functions, it should trust that agency to do its work based on its own expertise and experience, and avoid interfering to a great extent. But Representative Markey disagreed. Markey said that to the extent Congress acts, the agency must follow, "and when there is a consensus within Congress, short of legislation, the FCC also must comply with that consensus."[179]   The commission view on this was obviously different from the Congressional one.

Television Digest called August 4, 1987, a "red-letter day."[180]   At a regularly scheduled agenda meeting, the commission threw out the fairness doctrine on both constitutional and policy grounds.[181]   The commissioners, likening themselves to patriots upholding the Constitution, voted unanimously, 4-0, to end the agency's enforcement of the fairness doctrine.[182]   "Our action today should be cause for celebration," said chairman Dennis Patrick before a packed hearing room. "As we celebrate the bicentennial of our Constitution, it is especially fitting we affirm one of the Constitution's most fundamental principles--freedom of speech."[183] Acting Mass Media Bureau Chief, William Johnson, announced that "the few" fairness complaints pending would become "moot" immediately.[184]

Congressional leaders were incensed. "The American people, not the broadcasters, own the airwaves," said Ernest F. Hollings (D-South Carolina). "The threat today is that private interests, more motivated by profit than public interest, may limit public discourse."[185] Representative John Dingell accused the FCC of not keeping its word to Congress that its fairness doctrine alternatives report would be submitted to Congress before the commission acted. But minutes before agreeing to scrap the doctrine, the commission had voted to send its alternative report to Congress.[186] The Alternative Report considered a dozen "alternatives to doctrine short of complete elimination." The Report concluded "None of these alternatives was as desirable as complete elimination."[187]

In making the commission's case for repeal, general counsel Diane Killory said:

> We [the FCC staff] find that we are unable to analyze the doctrine from a pure policy public-interest perspective because the very purpose of the doctrine in the first place was to promote First Amendment values.   We find, therefore, that any policy justifications are so intertwined with constitutional implications that we cannot separate the two... It is time to heed the court's mandate and turn to the ... address ... whether the doctrine is constitutional. The answer is no.[188]

Though Killory was credited with the writing of the final fairness doctrine order, it was actually built on a base developed by Fowler, the commissioners, and a succeeding series of general counsels who preceded her. Killory, explained the production of the 76-page order was a joint effort between the Mass Media Bureau, and the General Counsel's Office. She thanked particularly Bill Johnson, Renee Licht, and Laurel Bergold of the Mass Media Bureau, and Richard Bozzelli, her special assistant.[189]

Television Digest quoted Patrick's response to congressional anger with the commission's actions:

Let me respond to those who suggest that the Commission should defer to Congress on this matter. To these critics I answer: We have. We deferred when we issued our fairness report almost two years ago and we deferred when [Meredith] first raised... constitutional challenge. But, there comes a point at which one must engage the issue, no matter how 'politically awkward'... Each member of the Commission has taken an oath to support and defend the Constitution. We believe that the evidence presented in our fairness inquiry and the record in this proceeding leads one inescapably to conclude that the fairness doctrine... contravenes the First Amendment and the public interest. As a consequence, we can longer impose fairness doctrine obligations on broadcasters and simultaneously honor our oath of office.[190]

The commission claimed that the congressional report language urging the commission delay, did not amount to a statutory directive. The only statutory requirement from Congress was the alternatives report, and its September 30, deadline. As *Broadcasting* said, "Technically speaking the FCC did forward its alternatives report to Congress before action on *Meredith*, if only by minutes."[191]

The 85-page Alternative Report was based on comments received in its Inquiry. As mentioned above, the Report suggested several ways the doctrine could be modified to make it "less objectionable than the present scheme when measured against public interest and constitutional requirements." But the Report made clear the commission position: "In sum, our analysis of these alternatives strengthens our belief that the fairness doctrine disserves the public interest and contravenes fundamental principles of free speech."[192]

The commission's decision on the fairness doctrine was fully supported by ex-chairman Fowler. He told *Broadcasting*, he saw no incongruity in the FCC's action and his past statements to Congress. "I don't see any conflict," Fowler said. "I think what they did was consistent with representation I made to Congress that we would not act on *Meredith* before we issued our report to Congress."[193] And he later told *Broadcasting*, of the commission's fairness action, "It's long overdue." He went on to say broadcasters should "show a little backbone and back the commission on this."[194]

Following the August 4 commission action, Patrick did try to ease the tension by personal visits to Senator Hollings and Representatives

Dingell and Markey. But as *Broadcasting* described it, "his overtures were rebuffed, and no meetings were held."[195]

On Thursday, August 6, *Television Digest* reported that the White House had settled on black attorney, Bradley Holmes, currently chief of FCC Mass Media Bureau's Policy and Rules Division, to fill the vacancy on commission that had existed since Fowler's resignation as chairman, April 17. However, *Television Digest*, citing unnamed congressional sources, said with the current foul mood of Congress toward the FCC, Holmes chances of confirmation were "slim to none." *Television Digest* claimed to have heard "Senate Democrats were considering holding up action on Holmes in retaliation for what they see as Patrick's and FCC's 'arrogance' in eliminating doctrine when bill to codify policy into law (S-742) was pending in Congress."[196]

Papers were filed, Saturday, August 8, in the Second U.S. Appeals Court, New York, on behalf of the Syracuse Peace Council. Syracuse was appealing the commission's reversal of its initial complaint. And, Syracuse said, it was prepared to argue that the agency lacked authority to repeal the fairness doctrine.[197] On behalf of the Syracuse, MAP filed a one-paragraph notice with the Court. MAP's notice argued that the fairness doctrine was compulsory, and that the commission "lacked the statutory authority to do what it did." Andrew Schwartzman, executive director of MAP, said the appeal was filed in the New York Appeals Court because: (1) New York was the home of Syracuse Peace Council; (2) The Second U.S. Appeals Court usually moves faster than the District of Columbia Court; and (3) the District of Columbia Court already had ruled (last September) that the doctrine is not codified into law.[198]

Commissioners quickly took to the stump to try and rally industry support for their action. In a speech to the West Virginia Broadcasters Association, the third week of August, commissioner James Quello warned that the "apathy" of broadcasters and "congressional indignation" would lead to the return of the fairness doctrine.[199] He prodded broadcasters, saying, "But the Packwood theory will probably prevail. Broadcasters can't lobby themselves out of a paper bag."[200]

But broadcasters did begin to gear up for a major fight on the fairness doctrine. NAB mounted a massive lobbying campaign to prevent Congress from reviving the fairness doctrine. The NAB was particularly concerned about blocking any fairness amendment before it becomes part of a larger legislative package.[201]

When the FCC repealed the fairness doctrine on August 4, it said that its action did not necessarily abolish the "corollaries" of the doctrine; the personal attack and political editorializing rules.   A group of broadcast and journalism associations, on Tuesday, August 25, asked the FCC to do away with these rules by "either clarifying its fairness doctrine action or by issuing an order in a four-year-old rulemaking that proposed elimination of the rules."[202]

The petitioners were the Radio-Television News Directors Association, the National Association of Broadcasters, the Media Institute, the Reporters Committee for the Freedom of the Press, the Society of Professional Journalists (Sigma Delta Chi) and Tribune Broadcasting Co. Their claim was, "The conclusion is inescapable that the FCC's personal attack and political editorial rules--adjuncts of the fairness doctrine and recognized to be even more intrusive and chilling than the general doctrine--are similarly unconstitutional and inimical to the public interest and accordingly must be eliminated forthwith."[203]

Postscript to 1987

As a direct result of the commission's August 4, fairness doctrine decision, the wheels of the Patrick commission's productive life ground to a halt. There were activities relative to the doctrine, both inside and outside the commission, which continued.   But the commission became so bogged down by congressional action it became virtually paralyzed.

There were numerous congressional attempts to get the doctrine codified. But the low agenda priority it had with most in Congress, the stand on principle by the Reagan Administration, and the effective lobbying by broadcasters, has kept the doctrine from ever making it to the floor of Congress for a vote. The bill has been introduced in every session of Congress since that time. And has always been passed successfully out of committee. But that is as far as it has ever gotten.

All court appeals to overturn the commission's decision also have failed. But even though the Appeals Court, District of Columbia, upheld the commission's authority to dismiss the doctrine, it never did rule on the doctrine's constitutionality.   And the Supreme Court rejected hearing the appeal without comment.   Though this can be viewed as a failure, in fact, the doctrine's constitutionality has never been overturned.   *Red Lion*'s determination of the doctrine's constitutionality is still the law of the land.

Returning now to the resulting paralysis of the commission, some further explanation is needed.   Following the resignation of Mimi Weyforth Dawson, on October 8, 1987, the commission became a three-member body.   It would remain that way until the summer of 1989 when President George Bush nominated his own slate of candidates for the commission.   Bush's slate included a new chairman, Al Sikes, to replace Dennis Patrick who had announced his resignation April 5, 1989.

Congress intentionally blocked the nomination hearings of both Bradley Holmes and Susan Wing.   Holmes had been nominated by Reagan on November 6, 1987, to the position left vacant by Mark Fowler's resignation.   Susan Wing was nominated by Reagan on December 11, 1987, to the position left vacant by the resignation of Dawson.   These two seats were of particular importance.   They were both Republican vacancies.   This gave those in Congress who control the nomination process even more leverage.   The Patrick commission was then composed of Republican Patrick, and two Democrats.

This epic, policy-and-turf struggle, between key congressional Democrats and President Reagan's appointees at the FCC, threw the agency into a policy-making grid-lock.   The standoff itself raises serious questions about the appropriate roles of Congress, and the FCC, in determining policy.

Until 1980 the FCC operated under a "permanent" congressional funding authorization.   This permanent authorization specified no fixed term and provided "such sums as may be necessary" for commission activities.   This provided for a degree of protection for the commission from political pressures.   Beginning in 1981, in a step taken to permit closer scrutiny of the agency, Congress shifted to a two-year authorization term.   But was scrutiny what was needed, or was it change?   So much of what occurred in the 1980's was a result of Congress' inability to effect any comprehensive changes to communications laws.   Rather than address communications issues collectively, Congress instead, did it piece-meal by attaching riders to authorization and appropriations measures to direct the FCC on specific policy matters.

Notes

1986

[1] "White House tentatively selects N.M. woman for FCC commissioner." *Television Digest*. January 13, 1986. 26:2. pp.1-2. At p.1.
[2] "Dennis said to be White House choice for FCC." *Broadcasting*. January 13, 1986. v.110. p.59.
[3] "Fairness doctrine elimination makes strange bedfellows." *Broadcasting*. January 20, 1986. v.110. p.222.
[4] Ibid.
[5] Ibid.
[6] *Meredith Corp. v. FCC*, 809 F.2d 863 (D.C. Cir. 1987).
[7] "Meredith wants a shot at the fairness doctrine: It thinks its appeal of FCC decision involving WTVH(TV) Syracuse is good case to test rule's constitutionality." *Broadcasting*. January 27, 1986. v.110. pp.32-3. At p.32.
[8] Ibid.
[9] *Miami Herald Publishing Co. v. Tornillo*, 418 U.S. 241 (1974).
[10] "Meredith wants a shot at the fairness doctrine: It thinks its appeal of FCC decision involving WTVH(TV) Syracuse is good case to test rule's constitutionality." *Broadcasting*. January 27, 1986. v.110. pp.32-3. At p. 32.
[11] Ibid.
[12] "Wirth eyes fairness doctrine." *Television Digest*. January 27, 1986. 26:4. p.7.
[13] "Reading the tea leaves at the FCC." *Broadcasting*. February 17, 1986. v.110. p.27.
[14] "Case presented against fairness doctrine: Broadcasters tell appellate court why they think doctrine and first amendment don't mix." *Broadcasting*. March 10, 1986. v.110. p.42.
[15] "Senate panel to propose shorter FCC member terms." *Television Digest*. March 10, 1986. 26:10. pp.1-2. At p.1.
[16] Ibid.
[17] "Nomination of Patricia Diaz Dennis to be a member of the Federal Communications Commission." Ronald Reagan. *Public Papers of the Presidents: Ronald Reagan: 1986*. U.S. Government Printing Office. Washington: 1988. March 11, 1986. p.321.

[18]Nominations--March--April, Hearings Before the Committee on Commerce, Science, and Transportation, U.S. Senate, 99th Congress, 2nd Session. On April 9, 1986, Patricia Diaz Dennis, To be a Commissioner, Federal Communications Commission, S. Hrg. 99-654.

[19]Ibid., at p.109.

[20]Ibid.

[21]Ibid., at pp.110-11.

[22]Ibid., at p.112.

[23]"Good news wins in Dallas. *Broadcasting*. April 21, 1986. v.110. pp.35-7. At p.35.

[24]Ibid., at p.36.

[25]"FCC chairman Fowler to be reappointed by White House." *Television Digest*. May 12, 1986. 26:19. pp.1-2. At p.1.

[26]Ibid.

[27]"FCC terms." *Congressional Quarterly Almanac*. 1986. p.290.

[28]"FCC terms shortened." *Television Digest*. May 26, 1986. 26:21. p.5.

[29]"Nomination of Mark S. Fowler to be a member of the Federal Communications Commission, and designation as chairman." Ronald Reagan. *Public Papers of the Presidents: Ronald Reagan: 1986*. U.S. Government Printing Office. Washington: 1988. June 5, 1986. p.725.

[30]"FCC terms." *Congressional Quarterly Almanac*. 1986. p.290.

[31]"Statement on signing the Federal Communications Commission bill." Ronald Reagan. *Public Papers of the Presidents: Ronald Reagan: 1986*. U.S. Government Printing Office. Washington: 1988. June 6, 1986. p.730.

[32]"FCC's resident comedian leaving for UCLA post after serving 2 chairmen." Howard Fields. *Television-Radio Age*. June 23, 1986. v.33. pp.109-10. At p.109.

[33]Ibid., at p.110.

[34]"NAB embraces public interest standard." *Television Digest*. June 23, 1986. 26:25. pp.2-4. At p.2.

[35]Ibid.

[36]"FCC has urged U.S. Court of Appeals in Washington to dismiss Meredith Broadcasting Corp.'s appeal of fairness doctrine complaint." *Broadcasting*. July 7, 1986. v.110. p.113.

[37]Making Continuing Appropriations for Fiscal Year 1987. Pub.L No. 99-500, signed into law on October 18, 1986. See also: Conference Report to Accompany H.J. Res. 738, H.R. Rep. No. 1005, 99th Congress, 2nd Session (1986).

[38]"Senate money bill loaded with policy: Committee adopts legislation on VHF-UHF swaps, fairness doctrine, international telecommunications policy committee in executive branch." *Broadcasting*. August 18, 1986. v.111. pp.40-1. At p.40.

[39]Ibid., at p.41.

[40]"Meredith presses on with fairness appeal: It asks appeals court to ignore FCC recommendation that fairness doctrine case be dismissed; it argues strongly that doctrine is unconstitutional." *Broadcasting.* August 25, 1986. v.111. pp.88,92. At p.88.

[41]*Telecommunications Research and Action Center v. FCC*, 801 F.2d 501 (D.C. Cir.), pet. for reh'g en banc denied, 806 F.2d 111 (D.C. Cir. 1986), cert denied, 55 U.S.L.W. 821 (U.S. 1987).

[42]"Limits put on fairness doctrine: FCC given freedom in 'teletext' usage." Ruth Marcus. *The Washington Post.* September 21, 1986.

[43]"Court opines on fairness doctrine." *Television Digest.* September 22, 1986. 26:38. p.5.

[44]Ibid.

[45]Report and Order in MM Docket No. 81-741, 48 Fed. Reg. 27054 (June 13, 1983).

[46]"Limits put on fairness doctrine: FCC given freedom in 'teletext' usage." Ruth Marcus. *The Washington Post.* September 21, 1986.

[47]Ibid.

[48]"Will FCC repeal fairness doctrine?: It may have power to do so, as appellate court implied, but Hill sends warning signals." *Broadcasting.* September 29, 1986. v.111. pp.72-3. At p.72.

[49]Ibid.

[50]Ibid., at p.73.

[51]"Appeals court troubled by FCC positions on fairness." *Television Digest.* October 6, 1986. 26:40. p.4.

[52]Ibid.

[53]Ibid.

[54]"Appeals court to FCC on fairness doctrine: If you don't like it, don't enforce it: Court gives signs of ducking constitutional question; presiding judge tells FCC it has power to repeal doctrine on public interest grounds." *Broadcasting.* October 6, 1986. v.111. pp.58-9. At p.58.

[55]"Public trustee concept in danger, say citizen groups: TRAC and MAP appeal recent court fairness doctrine decision, saying more regulation is called into question." *Broadcasting.* October 13, 1986. v.111. pp.77-8. At p.77.

[56]Making Continuing Appropriations for Fiscal Year 1987. Pub.L No. 99-500, signed into law on October 18, 1986. See also: Conference Report to Accompany H.J. Res. 738, H.R. Rep. No. 1005, 99th Congress, 2nd Session (1986).

[57]"Broadcasters block fairness doctrine codification." *Television Digest.* October 13, 1986. 27:40. pp.2-3. At p.3.

[58]"Quello calls for better journalism: He sees need for more emphasis on truth and responsibility; defends FCC's 'Steele' action." *Broadcasting*. October 13, 1986. v.111. pp.76-7. At p.76.

[59]"Legislative outlook: Reagan's sway over Congress slipping away." Stephen Gettinger. *Congressional Quarterly Weekly Report*. December 20, 1986. pp.3109-20. At p.3109.

[60]"The fairness doctrine is shackling broadcast." Hugh Carter Donahue. *Technology Review*. November-December 1986. v.89. pp.44-52. At p.46.

[61]"Fowler's obsession: Fighting the fairness doctrine." Herbert Dorfman. *The New Leader*. November 17, 1986. v.69. pp.9-11. At p.11.

[62]Ibid.

[63]*Telecommunications Research and Action Center v. FCC*, 801 F.2d 501 (D.C. Cir.), pet. for reh'g en banc denied, 806 F.2d 111 (D.C. Cir. 1986), cert denied, 55 U.S.L.W. 821 (U.S. 1987).

[64]"Ruling bolsters review of 'Fairness Doctrine': FCC seeks change in airing of views." Sandra Saperstain. *The Washington Post*. December 17, 1986.

[65]"Fairness doctrine another step closer to Supreme Court: Appeals court turns down request to rehear case in which judges held doctrine was policy, not law, that FCC could repeal; citizen group will probably appeal to high court." *Broadcasting*. December 22, 1986. v.111. pp.39-42. At p.41.

[66]"Ruling bolsters review of 'Fairness Doctrine': FCC seeks change in airing of views." Sandra Saperstain. *The Washington Post*. December 17, 1986.

[67]"The fairness doctrine: Law of the land or just FCC policy?" *Broadcasting*. December 22, 1986. v.111. pp.40-1. At p.40.

[68]Ibid.

[69]Ibid.

[70]Ibid.

[71]Ibid., at p.41.

[72]Ibid.

[73]"Fowler defends FCC policies." *Television Digest*. December 22, 1986. 26:51. p.5.

[74]Hearing Before the Subcommittee on Telecommunications and Finance, Committee on Energy and Commerce on H.R. 5373, H.R. 5651, U.S. House of Representatives, 99th Congress, 2nd Session. Serial No. 99-173. October 2, 1986.

[75]Ibid.

[76]"Legislative outlook: Reagan's sway over Congress slipping away." Stephen Gettinger. *Congressional Quarterly Weekly Report*. December 20, 1986. pp.3109-20. At p.3109.

1987

[77]"New Congress expected to mean greater oversight." *Broadcasting*. January 5, 1987. v.112. pp.164,166. At p.164.

[78]Ibid., at p.166.

[79]"FCC too far from public trustee concept, says Dingell: He feels marketplace philosophy has gone too far, calls for return to regulation in public interest." *Broadcasting*. January 19, 1987. v.112. pp.75-6. At p.75.

[80]"Dingell paves way for broadcast bill." *Television Digest*. January 19, 1987. 27:3. pp.3-4. At p.3.

[81]"FCC too far from public trustee concept, says Dingell: He feels marketplace philosophy has gone too far, calls for return to regulation in public interest." *Broadcasting*. January 19, 1987. v.112. pp.75-6. At p.76.

[82]First Amendment Clarification Act of 1987. S-22.

[83]"Fowler steps down after five years: Deregulation guru." *Variety*. January 21, 1987. v.325. pp.41,214. At p.214.

[84]"Fowler leaving in spring, Patrick on deck." *Television Digest*. January 19, 1987. 27:3. pp.1-2. At p.1.

[85]"Fowler steps down after five years: Deregulation guru." *Variety*. January 21, 1987. v.325. pp.41,214. At p.41.

[86]"Fowler makes final exit: Stage set for Patrick?" Linda M. Buckley and Carol Wilson. *Telephony*. January 26, 1987. v.212. p.12.

[87]"White House picks Patrick as chairman." *Broadcasting*. January 26, 1987. v.112. p.41.

[88]Ibid.

[89]"Fowler steps down after five years: Deregulation guru." *Variety*. January 21, 1987. v.325. pp.41,214. At p.214.

[90]Report Concerning General Fairness Doctrine Obligations of Broadcast Licensees, 102 FCC 2d 142 (1985), appeal pending sub nom. *Radio Television News Directors Association v. FCC*, No. 85-1691 (D.C. Cir. January 16, 1987).

[91]"FCC loses on fairness doctrine." *Television Digest*. January 19, 1987. 27:3. p.8.

[92]Ibid.

[93]*Meredith Corp. v. FCC*, 809 F.2d 863 (D.C. Cir. 1987). At. p.872,n.10.

[94]Ibid.

[95]*Syracuse Peace Council v. Television Stations WTVH*. FCC 87-33 (released Jan. 23, 1987).

[96]Ibid., at para.2. (Order Requesting Comments)

[97]"FCC aims at fairness doctrine." *Television Digest.* January 26, 1987. 27:4. p.3.

[98]Ibid.

[99]Ibid.

[100]"Designation of Dennis R. Patrick as chairman of the Federal Communications Commission." Ronald Reagan. *Public Papers of the Presidents: Ronald Reagan: 1987.* U.S. Government Printing Office. Washington: 1989. February 5, 1987. p.112.

[101]"Patrick designated FCC chairman." *Television Digest.* February 9, 1987. 27:6. pp.1-3. At p.1.

[102]Ibid., at p.2.

[103]"Its official: Patrick for FCC chairmanship; White House announcement accelerated by anti-pornography, pro-family campaign attacking incumbent commissioner." *Broadcasting.* February 9, 1987. v.112. pp.43-4. At p.44.

[104]"Patrick to face contentious Congress." Steven W. Colford. *Advertising Age.* February 16, 1987. v.58. p.28.

[105]"Campaigning is furious for FCC candidates." *Television Digest.* February 16, 1987. 27:7. pp.1-2. At p.1.

[106]"FCC candidates jockey in crowded field." *Broadcasting.* February 23, 1987. v.112. p.35.

[107]"Markey speaks out." *Television Digest.* February 9, 1987. 27:6. p.5.

[108]Ibid.

[109]Ibid.

[110]"Markey plans March hearing on fairness doctrine." *Television Digest.* February 16, 1987. 27:7. p.2.

[111]"Hollings plans broadcast bills." *Television Digest.* March 2, 1987. 27:9. pp.1-2. At p.1.

[112]Inquiry into Section 73.1910 of the Commission's Rules and Regulations Concerning Alternatives to the General Fairness Doctrine Obligations of Broadcast Licensees in MM Docket 87-26, 2 FCC Rcd 1532 (1987).

[113]Ibid.

[114]"Fowler faces hostile Senate panel." *Television Digest.* February 23, 1987. 27:8. pp.1-2. At p.1.

[115]Ibid., at p.2.

[116]"Fairness weighed in comments to FCC." *Broadcasting.* March 2, 1987. v.112. pp.39-40. At p.39.

[117]"Fairness doctrine rehearing asked." *Television Digest.* March 2, 1987. 27:9. p.4.

[118]Fairness in Broadcasting Act of 1987. S-742. See: Hearing Before the Subcommittee on Communications, Committee on Commerce, Science, and

Transportation on S.742. U.S. Senate, 100th Congress, 2nd Session. S.Hrg. 100-48. March 18, 1987.

[119]"Fairness doctrine bill offered in Senate." *Television Digest*. March 16, 1987. 27:11. pp.4-5. At p.4.

[120]Hearing Before the Subcommittee on Communications, Committee on Commerce, Science, and Transportation on S.742, U.S. Senate, 100th Congress, 1st Session. S.Hrg. 100-48. March 18, 1987.

[121]Ibid., at p.14.

[122]Freedom of Expression Act of 1987. S-827.

[123]"Fairness doctrine bill passed." *Television Digest*. March 30, 1987. 27:13. p.8.

[124]"New life to fairness doctrine repeal question." *Broadcasting*. March 23, 1987. v.112. p.54.

[125]"Emerging as front-runner." *Television Digest*. March 30, 1987. 27:13. p.8.

[126]Speech Before the National Association of Broadcasters, "Conclusion and Farewell." March 31, 1987. Dallas, Texas. In "The Federal Communications Commission 1981-1987: What the chairman said." *Hastings COMM/ENT Law Journal*. Winter 1988. Vol. 10. pp.409-500. At pp.417-20.

[127]"FCC eyeing property rights." *Television Digest*. April 6, 1987. 27:14. p.8.

[128]"The FCC according to Fowler: Chairman's tenure characterized by distrust of most regulation." Caroline E. Mayer and Elizabeth Tucker. *The Washington Post*. April 19, 1987.

[129]Ibid.

[130]"FCC launches assault on indecency." *Broadcasting*. April 20, 1987. 112:16. pp.35-6. At p.36.

[131]"Patrick picks up the reins at the FCC." Doug Haloren. *Broadcasting*. April 20, 1987. 112:16. pp.36-7. At p.36.

[132]Ibid., at p.37.

[133]Ibid.

[134]"Observers agree: Patrick can't avoid Fowler comparisons." *Television Digest*. April 20, 1987. 27:16. pp.1-3. At p.2.

[135]Ibid.

[136]"Patrick sets course for FCC." *Television Digest*. April 27, 1987. 27:17. pp.1-3. At p.1.

[137]Ibid.

[138]"Observers agree: Patrick can't avoid Fowler comparisons." *Television Digest*. April 20, 1987. 27:16. pp.1-3. At p.3.

[139]"Debate rages over the 'fairness doctrine.'" James E. Roper. *Editor & Publisher*. April 25, 1987. v.120. p.16.

[140]Hearing Before the Subcommittee on Telecommunications and Finance, Committee on Energy and Commerce on H.R. 1934. Broadcasters and the Fairness Doctrine, U.S. House of Representatives, 100th Congress, 1st Session. Serial No. 100-13. April 7, 1987.

[141]"White House eyeing veto of fairness doctrine bill." *Television Digest.* April 27, 1987. 27:17. pp.3-4. At p.4.

[142]"Patrick sets mass media priorities as FCC chairman." *Television Digest.* May 4, 1987. 27:18. pp.1-3. At p.1.

[143]Ibid., at p.2.

[144]Ibid.

[145]Ibid., at p.3.

[146]"Patrick era ushered in at FCC." *Broadcasting.* May 18, 1987. v.112. pp.45-6. At p.45.

[147]Ibid.

[148]Ibid.

[149]"Fairness bill ready to move to House floor: H.R. 1934 sweeps through Commerce Committee; administration's position on matter is still unclear." *Broadcasting.* May 18, 1987. v.112. p.77.

[150]"Broadcast bills advancing." *Television Digest.* May 18, 1987. 27:20. pp.4-5. At p.5.

[151]"Obscenity restrictions: Time, place and manner make the difference." *Television-Radio Age.* May 25, 1987. v.34. pp.77-8. At p.78.

[152]Ibid.

[153]Ibid.

[154]"Transportation/Commerce notes: 'Fairness Doctrine' sent to president." *Congressional Quarterly Weekly Report.* June 6, 1987. p.1197.

[155]"FCC veteran McKinney to join White House staff." *Television Digest.* June 15, 1987. 27:24. pp.1-2. At p.1.

[156]"McKinney move confirmed." *Television Digest.* June 22, 1987. 27:25. p.8.

[157]"FCC's Quello unequivocally says deregulation has 'gone too far'." *Variety.* June 17, 1987. v.327. pp.66,82. At p.66.

[158]Ibid.

[159]Ibid.

[160]*Telecommunications Research and Action Center v. FCC,* 801 F.2d 501 (D.C. Cir. 1986), reh'g den. December 16, 1986.

[161]"Veto seen for fairness doctrine bill." *Television Digest.* June 15, 1987. 27:24. p.2.

[162]"Patrick under the gun as House subcommittee pushes on fairness doctrine." *Television-Radio Age.* June 22, 1987. v.34. pp.103-4. At p.104.

[163]Ibid., at p.103.

[164]Ibid., at p.104.

[165]"Fairness doctrine on its way to White House." *Broadcasting*. June 8, 1987. v.112. pp.33-5. At p.33.

[166]"'Fairness' calls for a veto." (editorial) *The Washington Post*. June 10, 1987. p.A16.

[167]Ibid.

[168]"Veto seen for fairness doctrine bill." *Television Digest*. June 15, 1987. 27:24. p.2.

[169]"Message to the Senate returning without approval the Fairness in Broadcasting bill." Ronald Reagan. *Public Papers of the Presidents: Ronald Reagan: 1987*. U.S. Government Printing Office. Washington: 1989. June 19, 1987. pp.690-1. At p.690.

[170]Ibid., at p.691.

[171]Transcript. "White House chief of staff Howard Baker speech to the annual conference of the Radio and Television News Directors Association." Hyatt Regency, Capitol Hill, Washington, D.C., Friday, June 26, 1987.

[172]"Senate avoids override fight on 'Fairness Doctrine' veto: Democrats plan to repackage bill." Paul Starobin. *Congressional Quarterly Weekly Report* June 27, 1987. p.1401.

[173]"Senate ducks showdown over 'fairness' veto." Helen Dewar. *The Washington Post*. June 24, 1987. p.A5.

[174]Ibid.

[175]"Crying foul over fairness: Should the government require that broadcasting be balanced?" Richard Zoglin. *Time*. July 6, 1987. v.130. pp.80-1. At p.81.

[176]"Congress all fed up with runaway FCC: Full-time parent now." Howard Fields. *Television-Radio Age*. July 6, 1987. v.34. pp.40-2. At p.40.

[177]Ibid.

[178]Ibid., at p.41.

[179]Ibid.

[180]"FCC set to rule out fairness doctrine." *Television Digest*. August 3, 1987. 27:31. pp.1-3. At p.1.

[181]In Re Complaint of Syracuse Peace Council Against Television Stations WTVH, Syracuse, New York. Memorandum Opinion and Order. Adopted August 4, 1987. Released August 6, 1987.

[182]"FCC votes to end doctrine; options mulled." *Variety*. August 5, 1987. v.328. pp.1,56. At p.1.

[183]Ibid.

[184]"Unanimous FCC declares fairness doctrine unconstitutional." *Television Digest*. August 10, 1987. 27:31. pp.1-4. At p.1.

[185]"FCC rescinds 'Fairness Doctrine': Broadcasters hail end to 'intrusion'." Eleanor Randolph. *The Washington Post*. August 5, 1987.

[186]Ibid.

[187]In the Matter of Inquiry into Section 73.1910 of the Commission's Rules and Regulations Concerning Alternatives to the General Fairness Doctrine Obligations of Broadcast Licensees. Memorandum Opinion and Order. MM Docket No. 87-26, 2 FCC Rcd Vol 17 5272. FCC 87-264. Adopted August 4, 1987. Released August 4, 1987.

[188]"Decline and fall of the fairness doctrine: Fairness held unfair." (includes transcript of FCC proceedings) *Broadcasting*. August 10, 1987. v.113. pp.27(11). At p.30.

[189]Ibid., at p.29.

[190]"Unanimous FCC declares fairness doctrine unconstitutional." *Television Digest*. August 10, 1987. 27:31. pp.1-4. At p.3.

[191]"A question of priorities." *Broadcasting*. August 10, 1987. v.113. p.28.

[192]In the Matter of Inquiry into Section 73.1910 of the Commission's Rules and Regulations Concerning Alternatives to the General Fairness Doctrine Obligations of Broadcast Licensees. Memorandum Opinion and Order. MM Docket No. 87-26, 2 FCC Rcd Vol 17 5272. FCC 87-264. Adopted August 4, 1987. Released August 4, 1987. At p.5295.

[193]"A question of priorities." *Broadcasting*. August 10, 1987. v.113. p.28.

[194]"Former FCC commissioners divided over fairness move." *Broadcasting*. August 24, 1987. v.113. pp.64-5.

[195]"Unmended fences." *Broadcasting*. August 10, 1987. v.113. p.10.

[196]"Bradley Holmes to be named to FCC seat vacated by Fowler." *Television Digest*. August 10, 1987. 27:31. pp.4-5. At p.4.

[197]"Syracuse group protests dumping of fairness doc; Dems map counterattack." Paul Harris. *Variety*. August 12, 1987. v.328. p.52.

[198]"Fairness doctrine action appealed." *Television Digest*. August 17, 1987. 27:32. p.4.

[199]"Quello urges broadcasters to get behind fairness repeal." *Broadcasting*. August 24, 1987. v.113. pp.65-6. At p.65.

[200]Ibid.

[201]"Broadcasters arming themselves for uphill fairness fight: NAB and state associations find their work cut out for them in convincing congressmen to oppose codification of fairness rules." *Broadcasting*. August 31, 1987. v.113. pp.36-7. At p.36.

[202]"Petitioners ask FCC to ax fairness doctrine corollaries." *Broadcasting*. August 31, 1987. v.113. p.89.

[203]"Media groups turn to FCC." *Television Digest*. August 31, 1987. 27:35. pp.1-2. At p.1.

CHAPTER VI

ANALYSIS AND CONCLUSIONS

Analysis

The research question raised here was, how did the FCC from 1981 to 1987, through reorganization, procedural reform, change in mandate, and alterations to its external environment, position itself so as to relieve itself of its obligation to enforce the broadcast fairness doctrine? These four concepts have concomitant effect, but I will address them separately here for the purpose of discussion.

Reorganizational Changes

Were there reorganizational changes that affected the final result, e.g. dismissal of the fairness doctrine? There were actually a number of them. Some, such as reducing the number of commissioners and the length of their terms, came from outside the agency. But probably the most significant reorganizational changes came from within the commission. The creation of the new Mass Media Bureau was probably the most significant reorganizational change. This new bureau combined the former Broadcast and Cable Bureaus, as well as other responsibilities previously handled by the Common Carrier Bureau. All of the various responsibilities were now folded into one bureau. By combining into one bureau responsibility for regulating technologies previously guided in regulation by three distinct models, the traditional broadcast regulation model, and its underlying rationales were called into question. Effectively, through reorganization, broadcasting became only one technology among many. And its underlying justifications were made suspect.

Though there were also a number of other reorganizational changes which occurred, one other bears mentioning here. That was the changed role of the general counsel. Prior to Fowler, the general counsel acted as the chairman's and the commission's legal advisor. The general counsel offered legal opinion and advice on pending commission matters. But under Fowler, this position assumed a major policy role. Bruce Fein, in particular, was known for the advocacy he brought to the position. And, it was his language in the commission's teletext decision that ultimately allowed the Patrick commission to claim legitimacy in throwing the doctrine out in 1987.

Procedural Reforms

Procedural reforms affect administrative law, legal precedent, and the operating rules of an agency. How did procedural reforms affect the commission with respect to the fairness doctrine? One way is mentioned above. The commission's rule that teletext, which uses licensed broadcast frequencies, was not subject to fairness obligations. The commission chose to constrain its own decision-making power. There are actually too many procedural reforms enacted during this period to mention them all here. But a few of the most significant ones will be cited.

Possibly the most significant procedural reform resulted from the commission's 1985 Fairness Report. The commission began its fairness inquiry in 1983 claiming it was only gathering information for future decisions. But ultimately, both the commission, and the Courts, used the resulting Report as though it were a final determination. The conclusions of this report provided the commission with an agency document questioning the constitutional basis of the doctrine. Though the doctrine has never been ruled unconstitutional, the commission, industry groups and the courts, have been provided with a powerful tool to argue against the doctrine.

There were also a number of court cases the commission drew on to build its case against the fairness doctrine. Most influential were the *League of Women Voters*, and the *TRAC* cases. Though these cases were not of the scope of the 1969 *Red Lion* decision, they did serve as a means of keeping attention focused on the fairness issue. They also served as examples of a direction shift within the judicial system. The commission would never have achieved its goal without a pronounced conservative swing in the courts.

Two final documents representing procedural reforms also deserve mention here. These were, first, the 1987 Memorandum Opinion and Order dismissing the doctrine, and second, the Alternatives Report. These are important because, as conditions exist today, they are still the final word on the doctrine.

Changing the Mandate

Perhaps no other type of reform was more effectively used by the commission than changing its mandate. Although, statutorily, the commission's mandate to regulate in "the public interest, convenience or necessity" did not change, the meaning of this phrase changed drastically. It was this redefinition of terms, that served as the very basis for almost all of the commission's actions respecting the fairness doctrine during this time.

Mark Fowler immediately claimed the terms of the debate. He did so by redefining the term public interest. His definition of public interest sought to remove, to the extent possible, social responsibility from the agency. Instead, he changed the meaning of the term public interest protected the interests of the regulated industries. Fowler did much the same thing when he equated marketplace theory, an economic theory, with Milton's democratic notion of marketplace of ideas.

Though many in Congress disagreed with these redefinitions, Fowler had the support of the Reagan Administration, key Republican Congressional leaders, and many Reagan appointed justices. Though the above criticism focuses on Fowler's notion of marketplace of idea, it also must be pointed out that even Fowler's idea of the economic marketplace was not universally accepted. For example, MCI Chairman William G. McGowan, said that the FCC commissioners and staff members:

> [D]on't really understand the marketplace, and they don't understand capital formation. Most of them have never operated a business—they're all economists and attorneys obsessed with an economic theory that bears little relation to reality.[1]

Altering the External Environment

As already mentioned, the commission's statutory mandate did not change. Yet it was still able to effect the dismissal of the doctrine. One way this was accomplished was the very visible role Mark Fowler, and to a lesser extent the other commissioners, took in advocating its dismissal. Fowler narrowly identified his public, and he lobbied for their support continuously. Though traditionally the FCC chairman gives numerous public speeches, Mark Fowler is credited with well over 200 public addresses. Fowler recognized that by himself he would never be able to get Congress to dismiss the fairness doctrine-- although there were a minority of powerful Congressmen who like Fowler opposed it. So Fowler took his call public. And he kept it public his entire term.

Conclusions

Charles Ferris, who preceded Fowler as chairman, had goals when he assumed the chair of the commission. But Fowler took office with an even more clearly defined set of goals. Not only that, he had firm objectives which he believed would achieve them. In fact, one of the reasons Fowler ran into frequent Congressional roadblocks, was because he did propose such sweeping changes. Previous chairmen were more cautious and more politically adept at fashioning rules that moved toward deregulation in small steps, rather than big leaps.

Both Fowler and Patrick had explosive relationships with Congress. But Fowler's can not be explained solely in terms of his own stubbornness. Ferris, who began the agency move toward deregulation, had already established a negative relationship with Congress. Fowler inherited an agency that had been gradually encouraging more competition in industries, such as video and long-distance telephone service. And as a result, more businesses and trade associations were created that applied competitive (and anti-competitive) pressures on both the commission and Congress. As those industries grew in economic importance, FCC policies were transformed from back-page issues to front-page news, assuring a higher profile for commission activities.

The added pressures and media attention were also partially responsible for increased scrutiny from congressional committees overseeing the FCC, as well as from other members of Congress who saw political advantage in attacking commission decisions. Hollings, Dingell and Wirth, as well as Packwood, Goldwater, and Proxmire all had reputations as being politically aggressive. And much like Fowler, they liked to air their gripes publicly.

The FCC also was not totally unique to the time. Other independent agencies like the National Labor Relations Board, the Equal Employment Opportunity Commission, and the Nuclear Regulatory Commission, just to name a few of the independent boards and commissions that managed much of the government's regulatory business, all became Ronald Reagan's agencies.

These are all independent bodies, whose original mandates had them operating behind barriers erected by Congress to shield them from direct presidential control. But in the 1980's the individuals running these independent agencies were virtually all Reagan appointees. According to a 1985 *National Journal* article, of the 63 sitting members of the 15 key independent regulatory agencies, 58 were Reagan appointees.[2]

As a group, Reagan's regulators transformed the character of these independent agencies. His regulators had been selected from a very different pool than President Carter's. Carter had selected activists from congressional staffs or public interest groups. Reagan chose industry officials and academics who disdained the regulatory activism of the 1970s.

So the FCC was not totally unique. But it was a good example. In fact, *Business Week* characterized Fowler's commission this way in 1985:

> Under [Fowler's] antic leadership, the federal agency charged with overseeing the booming broadcasting and telecommunications industries has become Washington's most advanced laboratory for the antiregulatory theories of the Reagan Administration.

Unlike the Civil Aeronautics Board, which deregulated itself out of existence at the behest of Congress, the FCC is deregulating itself into one of the most important agencies in Washington.[3]

Understanding the role broadcasters played is also important. Broadcasters applauded early commission moves to deregulate their industry. Their welcome of Fowler, as chairman, may in fact have been unprecedented in recent commission history. But by 1986, the implications of the shift in the FCC's view of its own role--from a guardian of the public interest to an indifferent bystander in private business disputes--seriously disturbed broadcasters. As they began to see that Fowler's idea of competition negatively impacted their operations, they began to move much more cautiously. Fowler did not always grasp their actions, nor did he ever fully let on he understood their motivations.

What the fairness doctrine actually was became an early casualty of the Fowler term. It became, in Willard Rowland's term, reified. Fowler claimed the fairness doctrine was "Orwellian," and drew analogies between it and Nazi Germany. Others, though, saw it less onerously. For them it was not an all-or-nothing proposition. These interpretations were based on the experience that, in practice, the fairness doctrine exacted only marginal concessions from most broadcasters. From this perspective broadcasters retained their first amendment rights to have their own say on the air, while allowing others to stand on the same soapbox. This was an argument Fowler dismissed. Maybe someday a reasoned discussion can occur that again locates some true meaning of the term. But reasoned discussion is not what occurred between 1981 and 1987.

One final note is also in order. In countless public forums, Mark Fowler emphasized the fact that a goal of his was to bring rationality to the policy-making process. The historical record which exists, relative to the commission's activity regarding the fairness doctrine, certainly proves that Fowler knew how to act purposefully. But, I suspect his redefinition of the term rationality would disavow reasoned argument and dialectic exchange. So, even though I will certainly grant Fowler credit for being purposeful, and bringing purposefulness to the policy-making process, I am not willing to credit him with bringing rationality to the policy-making process.

Notes

[1]"Has the FCC gone too far? Even fans of deregulation say chairman Fowler is rushing things." John Wilke, Mark Vamos and Mark Maremont. *Business Week*. August 5, 1985. pp.48-54. At p.52.

[2]"Regulatory agencies: Reagan's regulators." Ronald Brownstein, Richard E. Cohen, Ann Cooper, Richard Corrigan, Rochelle L. Stanfield and Bruce Stokes. *National Journal*. May 18, 1985. pp.1188-1200. At p.1188.

[3]"Has the FCC gone too far? Even fans of deregulation say chairman Fowler is rushing things." John Wilke, Mark Vamos and Mark Maremont. *Business Week*. August 5, 1985. pp.48-54. At p.48.

INDEX